LISTEN!
SAY YES!
COMMIT!

LISTEN! SAY YES! COMMIT!

Listen! Say Yes! Commit!

Improvisation for Communication, Creativity, Teamworking
and Leadership at Work

Harry Puckering and Julia E Knight

LISTEN! SAY YES! COMMIT!

First published in 2015 by Harry and Julia Improv

ISBN 978-1-326-12849-4

www.harryandjuliaimprov.com

A catalogue record for this book is available from the British Library

Table of contents

Exercises by chapter

Chapter 2: Communication

- Repeat before you reply
- Elevator pitch / cocktail party chat
- Observation repeat conversation
- Customer service
- Loud business meeting
- Limericks
- Writing and reading a diary
- Reading prose and poetry aloud
- Recording yourself

Chapter 3: Creativity

- Free association / layering associations
- Brain gym
- Point and name
- Rolodexing
- Structured brainstorming
- Yes and...
- Analogies and Word association
- Lists
- Sentence completion
- Machines
- Physical layout
- Metaphors
- If it's bad make it worse!

Chapter 4: Teamworking

- Share your stuff
- Pass the clap / click
- Sevens
- Pattern games
- Walk-stop-jump
- Word-at-a-time story
- One to twenty
- Yes Let's!
- Playground game
- Point-a-story
- Freeze tag
- Bodyguard / enemy or Safety zone
- Chairs

Chapter 5: Leadership

- Roleplaying
- Machines (reprise)
- Three-line conversations
- Blank workplace
- Status games
- Museum curator
- Press conference
- Story line
- Colour advance
- Super managers
- Elevator pitch / cocktail party chat (reprise)

Acknowledgements

Harry and Julia would like to thank Heather Urquhart, Katy Schutte, Jenny Rowe, Jason Delplanque and all The Maydays, but especially John Cremer, for inspiration, examples and training.

Harry would like to apologise for being grumpy in other people's improv training events. He expresses his sincere thanks to present and past members of The Hee-Ha's for letting him be himself, and other people. And he is especially thankful to Maggie, Molly and Ruby for letting him witter on endlessly about improv.

Julia would like to apologise for being grumpy generally. She expresses sincere thanks to Hee-Ha's past and present for support, love and many hours of improv fun. She is especially thankful to Tony for accompanying her to improv gigs wherever and whenever requested and for being willing to discuss 'first love' on their second date.

Harry and Julia would like to thank our Editor, Zosia Williams, and Dr Kamal Birdi, Karyn Boots, Carra Bosworth, Ian Florance, Gene Johnson, and Alison Temperley, who read and reviewed pre-publication versions of this book. All their comments and suggestions made the book far better. Any remaining problems are entirely the responsibility of Harry and Julia.

Foreword

The quickly changing landscape of the 21st Century is offering so many challenges for modern organisations that it is no longer sustainable to keep on doing the same old things. Success will instead be much more strongly influenced by having greater flexibility, creativity, collaboration and dynamic leadership. The ability to improvise plays a key role in all these fundamental aspects and it is something that organisations need to be better at doing. In over twenty years of researching and working with organisations, I have come across very few that are truly comfortable in breaking free of established roles and boundaries to allow creative exploration and co-operation.

I was therefore very pleased when I read *LISTEN! SAY YES! COMMIT!* as it offers an excellent resource for those wanting to effectively introduce improvisational activities into the workplace. Harry and Julia bring their extensive experience to bear in a very readable way. It is great to see a mix of practitioner advice backed up with useful insights from academic research into how improvisation functions. I am particularly impressed with the sheer range of improvisation exercises provided to help develop the key domains of communication, creativity, teamworking and leadership. You will have no shortage of different approaches to try out! This is an approachable book for anyone looking to meaningfully freshen up the way their organisation works.

Dr Kamal Birdi C. Occ. Psychol.
Senior Lecturer in Occupational Psychology
Institute of Work Psychology
The Management School
University of Sheffield

LISTEN! SAY YES! COMMIT!

Introduction

How to use this book

Harry and Julia planned this book to make the content accessible and useable by a range of people including managers of teams, facilitators, trainers and change agents, as well as individuals with an interest in developing their own creativity and that of the people around them.

The chapters are arranged in such a way as to offer clear pointers to the content, making it easy to dip into the relevant sections as and when you need to. Do be aware, however, that there is a progression to the book: the earlier chapters provide a foundation upon which the later ones sit, so please don't attempt to run before you can walk! Even if you are focused on team development, have a skim through the chapters on communication and creativity first. As we emphasise throughout the book, developing improvisation skills requires practice, so build up slowly.

Please note that the exercises we describe in this book are not our property: they are drawn from what we have been taught and from our experiences as trainers, facilitators and learners. You may well come across the same or similar exercises in other improvisational training or publications. As Kat Koppett (2001) says, it is nigh on impossible to trace the original source of any individual exercise.

Planning improvisation sessions

If you are planning to facilitate or lead a session with a group, we recommend thinking about and setting your objectives carefully, then building a structure designed to achieve them.

When working with groups and teams with no prior experience of our approach, we often include the basic objective 'to practise some improvisation exercises and discuss how these are relevant to our/their work'.

We think that it is important for the facilitator to role-model the principles of improvisation (improv) during the session itself, so by all means have a plan, but be prepared to adjust this to the group by listening to them, saying yes, and committing to their needs. If you have experience of improvising, be prepared for the group to be a long way behind you in terms of speed of processing. Take it slowly. Take time to debrief each exercise, and be aware that the group will get tired more quickly than you might expect because they are doing something very new to them.

Encouraging participation

In pure improv workshops unconnected to workplaces, it is typical to have a 'no observers' policy. If you attend the workshop you should be prepared to join in with most activities.

In the workplace this can sometimes be difficult because events and workshops are not always entirely voluntary (even if badged as such). We have come to the conclusion that there is little point forcing those who are extremely uncomfortable to join in. However, we have also found that setting clear parameters at the start of the workshop maximises participation.

We tell people that we would prefer everyone to take part and that pushing themselves outside their comfort zone is part of the experience, but we also say they can step out at any time if they really don't feel comfortable.

We also tend to structure our workshops so that the first exercises are carried out in pairs, and subsequent exercises involve the whole group. In our experience, the exercises that people tend to find more challenging are those where they are 'performing' in front of the rest of the group as if on stage. When we are working with a group for the first time, we always use those exercises towards the end of the session, and only with volunteers.

Always bear in mind what the group is there for. If they have signed up for a 'thinking on your feet' workshop, they should expect to feel at least a little 'on the spot' at times. Your role as facilitator is to create a safe environment where they feel comfortable in doing so. The great thing about improvisation is that there isn't a wrong way to do it!

Tips

- Tell people they are doing well at regular intervals.
- Use positive words ('excellent', 'brilliant', 'fantastic') often.
- Reward mistakes – mistakes make improv great.
- (Most importantly) have fun!

Chapter 1: Why Improv?

There are already loads of books and other resources about theatrical and comedy improvisation, and a few about improvisation in organisations: please look at our reference list and bibliography at the end of this book.

So why have Harry and Julia written another? Here are the main reasons:

- We haven't found a short, useful, recent, UK-authored guide to improv for trainers, facilitators, coaches, leaders, managers or business and work psychologists who want to use improv ideas, exercises, theories and research evidence in their day jobs.
- We haven't found enough material grounded in and built on the strong and growing British improv community, especially the Brighton improv community.
- We haven't found anything based on a thorough and eclectic international literature review.
- We haven't found much that emphasises that it is the extended practice of improv that yields the greatest benefits. Improv contains lots of nice ideas and great things to do, but if they are considered or tried out once or twice, they don't make much difference. If they are repeated and practised frequently and regularly, they can become embedded in behaviour and trained into unconscious thinking, and thus change the people, teams and organisations where they are practised.
- We love improv and we want to move it forward.

Our approach is a little different from that of most of the more popular and commonly referenced improv texts. We're not primarily directors or improvisational actors. We are not focused on improvisation performance. Instead, we have for many years provided consultancy services and designed and delivered learning events and programmes to organisations that want to do what they do better. Over that time, we have come to believe that frequently and regularly practising improv as part of wider learning and development is a good way (but not by any means the only way) to improve communication, creativity, teamwork and leadership. And that this can work at individual, team and organisational levels.

Organisations have been interested in improvisation for some time, and interest appears to be on the increase, as the ability to adapt and change has become essential. Organisations have become increasingly aware of the relevance of improvisation to organisational success.

'In the past decade, improvisation has gained recognition as a strategic competence that supports 21st-century firms' requirements for change, adaptability, responsiveness to the environment, loose boundaries, and minimal hierarchy' (Vera and Crossan, 2004)

But what do we mean when we talk about 'improvisation'? Here are some definitions:

Why Improv?

In theatre:

'True improvisation is getting on-stage and performing without any preparation or planning... improvisation is making it up as you go along' (Halpern et al., 1994)

'Improvisation is a mixture of "making do" and "letting go"' (Seham, 2001)

In organisations:

'...the degree to which composition and execution converge in time' (Moorman and Miner, 1998)

'...conception of action as it unfolds, by an organisation and/or its members, drawing on available material, cognitive, affective and social resources' (Kamoche et al., 2003)

'The creative and spontaneous process of trying to achieve an objective in a new way' (Vera and Crossan, 2005)

A definition we like is *'the mindful application of a few simple rules of thumb to new circumstances in order to generate spontaneous behaviour'*.

We've said what improv is. Next we'll talk about what we don't mean by improvisation... stand-up comedy.

Stand-up comedy

To an outsider, there can seem to be strong similarities between improv and stand-up. They are both funny (or at least can be). They happen on stages with minimal sets, costumes and props. BUT... with the exception of a handful of near geniuses (Robin Williams, Billy Connolly, Eddie Izzard and Ross Noble spring to mind) who seem to create and riff off the audience and the environment in real time, stand-up is usually:

- scripted and rehearsed
- performed solo
- based on conflict and victimisation
- adversarial in its treatment of the audience.

In comparison, improv is:

- made up in the moment and ephemeral
- broadly positive and 'kindly' in approach
- created and performed in collaboration with other performers and with the audience.

So stand-up is almost a model for bad leadership and management, while improv is a model for best practice. That's also why improv works as development in organisations.

Denial and blocking

We'll talk more about denial and blocking in the chapters that follow, but to introduce it briefly here, denial and blocking is what happens when we don't listen, say yes or commit to the people around us or the situation we are in. It's the opposite of good communication, creativity, teamworking and leadership. And it's interesting, because it's so obviously bad for people, for teams and organisations, even though it happens everywhere. And it's so easy to spot in others but so hard to spot or stop in ourselves. And it manifests in so many different and various ways: ignoring, forgetting, boredom, complacency, tiredness, inauthenticity, censoring, criticising, punchlining, putdowns, sarcasm, 'joking'... And it seems to come from so many sources: evolution, physiology, psychology, societal development, ideology, philosophy and belief, common practice and expectations.

As improvisers, we try not to block or deny others. In our work, we try to anticipate, identify, address and change blocking and denial. We look at it again and again. And it looks bad: aggressive or passive or passive-aggressive, rude, uncreative, uncollaborative and unfunny.

But stand-up behaviour often looks good. It's funny, so stand-ups think they are good improvisers because they are making people laugh. But while they are trying to trump the action or ideas around them in their heads, composing the perfect put-down or punchline, they are NOT listening, or saying yes or committing.

Feature: The need for improvisation in organisations

The worldwide organisational and business environment now seems to involve unavoidable, accelerating speed of change and increasing uncertainty. The typical reaction of businesses and other organisations often emphasises planning, formalisation, compliance and systematisation as a means to an end, through industry-spanning enterprise software such as those from SAP and Oracle.

People at work seem to be finding the rules more definite, even while they have to be able to decide, act and change faster, think on their feet, and manage in a more ambiguous and complex social environment. Matrix management, broad flat teams, flexible working and the rise of outworkers, contractors and organisational alliances require leaders, managers and almost everyone else to have greater authenticity and social skills in dealing with others. Teams need to be (re)formed and (re)built quickly. Connections need to be made easily and deeply. The new needs to be picked up and assimilated, while the old needs to be dropped and forgotten.

Communicating effectively with others is vital in one-to-one and group contexts, especially when people have neither the time nor the resources to plan the message or methods in advance. People and teams need to practise creative problem solving while increasing buy-in among team members.

Vera and Crossan (2005) provide a useful framework

18

that outlines the conditions where improvisation is important in organisations. They base the model on the idea that improvisation contains elements of both creativity and spontaneity, but that these elements can exist independently. They further relate these elements to the levels of uncertainty and time pressure present, as shown in the diagram below.

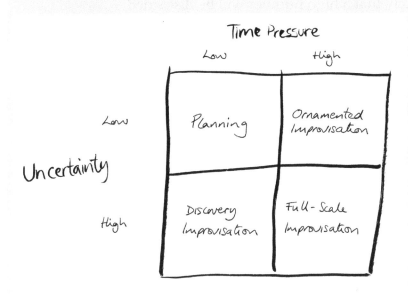

Planning. Under conditions of low uncertainty and low time pressure, managers do not need to be creative or spontaneous, as detailed analysis and planning will be the effective way to deal with their environment.

Ornamented improvisation. Where there is a need to respond urgently, a planning approach will probably be insufficient; responding in the moment becomes vital. This type of improvisation is characterised by a high level of spontaneity, but there is less need to be creative, as the environmental cues are clear.

Discovery improvisation. Uncertainty in the environment is high, but time pressure is low, so improvisation is characterised by high levels of creativity, as individuals try out different ideas, utilising past knowledge. The ideas can be evaluated later and it is likely that a high number will be discarded

Full-scale improvisation. A situation where time is scarce and the environment unpredictable is often going to be a crisis. If individuals decide to use an improvising approach they can 'wade into situations with fallible knowledge, secure in the belief that they can recombine that knowledge by shifting their fallibilities around. Faith in their ability to "make do" infuses confidence into their balance of knowledge and doubt' (Weick, 1998).

Background and historical roots of improv

The roots of improv can be traced back to traditions of oral histories and storytelling in ancient civilisations, to Greek tragedy and the Commedia dell'arte of the 16th century, but the modern form did not take shape until the 1960s with Viola Spolin's creation of Second City in Chicago, and Keith Johnstone's Theatresports in the UK. This makes improv a relatively young theatre form.

Important milestones, people and groups in improv history

- Oral history and storytelling
- Greek tragedy
- Commedia dell'arte

20

Why Improv?

- Pantomime; Punch and Judy; Grand Guignol
- Joan Littlewood and Theatre Workshop
- Keith Johnstone: Royal Court, then Canada (he called it 'impro' rather than 'improv')
- Canadian improv: Loose Moose Theatre Company; Theatresports
- Chicago improv: Viola Spolin and Second City; IO (formerly ImprovOlympic); Annoyance Theatre
- New York improv: Upright Citizens Brigade
- Los Angeles improv: The Groundlings
- Whose Line is it Anyway?
- UK troupes: London, Brighton and Bristol
- Actors' use of improv
- Writers' use of improv
- Improv in today's media e.g. Fast and Loose, Paul Merton's Impro Chums

Please Google these to find out what they are and what people say about them.

Short-form and long-form improvisation

Comedy and theatrical improvisers often differentiate between short-form and long-form improvisation.

Short-form is composed of short scenes and games that are introduced, explained and ended ('Cut!' or 'Scene!') by an MC. The improvisers' only responsibility is to follow the truth and internal logic of the scene and stay committed to the character they've chosen ('Don't drop your shit!'). Short-form can be very successful and entertaining, gag-based and slick, partly because the improvisers can focus on improvisation and leave the management and editing to the MC. This is where you can really see 'rehearsed spontaneity' at work (see later in this chapter).

In long-form there is no MC and no separate games or scenes. Instead the improvisers manage the beginnings, transitions and ends of scenes themselves, seemingly often without any explicit verbal agreement about how this will happen (but actually with a good deal of prior practice). The best long-form groups use all the possible transitions seen in movies, novels and comic books. Doing so 'on the fly' and without discussions and agreements between improvisers involves the building up of 'group mind' through theatre training techniques. Long-form is where 'collective individualism' really comes into its own (see later in this chapter).

The key skills a performer needs to create successful long-form improv seem to match those of a film editor rather than those of a writer or director; long-form improv requires a sense of structure and flow, and an ability to spot when to start and stop. These skills may also be the essential competency in the management and leadership of modern businesses; rather than planning or controlling the work of teams, or blindly 'just doing the job', great managers need to know roughly where the business has come from and is going, and to have the confidence and ability to direct attention toward what's important.

If you are interested in finding out more about improv, we have listed several books in the bibliography. If you want to find out about improv classes in the UK, see The Crunchy Frog Collective website.

Feature: What can we learn from improvisers?

Music and theatre are both areas associated with the concept of improvising. There is a fair amount of writing that has borrowed concepts from jazz improvisation to inform organisational theory. Much of this writing uses jazz improvisation as a metaphor for organisational life. Improvisation is also something that is utilised in the theatre arts, and authors have examined the similarities between theatrical improvisation and organisational life. While there is not a huge literature specifically related to the actual use of theatrical improvisation as a tool within organisations, there are a few articles and some evidence of the trainability and transferability of improv skills to teams at work.

Improvisation as metaphor: lessons from jazz

In 1998, Organization Science dedicated a whole edition to papers that discussed the lessons to be learned by organisations from jazz improvisation. What is most useful about these discussions are the concepts they identify. These ideas attempt to understand the process of jazz improvisation and then relate this to work situations.

In his paper 'Variations on a Theme—Practice Improvisation' in that edition, Philip Mirvis provides a set of paradoxes that he believes underpins successful improvisation in jazz, and argues that these paradoxes are highly relevant to organisations. The concept of paradox in organisations has been talked about elsewhere, most notably by Chris Argyris, who sees the acknowledgement and study of behavioural paradox as essential to understanding organisations (1985, 1999).

Mirvis outlines four paradoxes drawn from jazz which, if acknowledged and embraced, he believes could be key to harnessing the power of improvisation in business: rehearsed spontaneity, anxious confidence, collective individualism and planned serendipity.

Rehearsed spontaneity
Improvisers (in jazz and theatre alike) create their outputs spontaneously on stage, but behind that is a huge amount of previous rehearsal. It is necessary to spend time practising the process, to understand what works and how elements can be put together to create a coherent performance.

Mirvis says: 'Regular practice in dealing with the tension between following a prearranged plan versus adjusting to the exigencies of the moment helps individuals and groups to get comfortable with the notion of improvising and gives them comparatively low-risk experience doing so.'

So, practising having to think on their feet will help individuals to be more successful when situations requiring that behaviour arise at work.

Anxious confidence
This paradox relates to the need to be at a certain level of arousal in order to be motivated by the task, but not so anxious or over-confident that performance is impaired. Mirvis compares this to the concept of 'eustress' and also to Csikszentmihalyi's flow states.

In relation to flow, the balance between challenge and anxiety is key to achieving the state. Too little challenge to an individual's skills can result in boredom, too much and anxiety takes over. Achieving flow more often at work is associated with higher reported levels of overall satisfaction and feelings of motivation (see Csikszentmihalyi, 1990).

Collective individualism

In a jazz ensemble there is no formal leader. Each player takes a turn at being the leader (doing their solo), then drops back into the group. To the outsider, this appears to happen without any obvious direction. This moving in and out of leading and following as a team member is a key skill in good improvising.

In today's more complex organisations, where an individual may work as a member of several teams, the ability to understand how and when to contribute is an important skill.

Planned serendipity

This concept is concerned with the tension between the need for freedom in order to allow creativity, and the need to maintain control. This paradox occurs almost as a product of the other three. Improvisers who seem both rehearsed and spontaneous, both anxious and confident, both collective/collaborative and individual, seem to produce the best improvisation as if by accident. If they are asked 'Where did that come from?', they'll often say that they don't know. Mirvis contends that the pairing of 'tight and loose' is key to long-term learning in organisations.

So, concepts generated from studying jazz improvisation

are relevant and applicable to organisations, and we very much like these paradoxes. However, the difficulty with jazz is that it is so specialised and not very accessible to most people (even other musicians!). This is probably why organisational interest moved to improvisation in the theatre. While theatre (or comedy) improvisation shares many features with jazz, it does not depend on a specialised skill set. Everyone has access to the tools of improv – speech, gesture, facial expression etc. – so they can take it beyond the level of metaphor. In addition, the methods that actors use to learn to improvise can be transferred directly into organisations. And it's fun!

Chapter 2: LISTEN! Work on Communication

Harry and Julia, like many other trainers and business psychologists, often find themselves asking their clients: 'What would you most like to improve in your organisation?' Or: 'Where are your biggest obstacles or barriers to working effectively?' Or perhaps: 'Why do you think you aren't hitting your productivity or profitability targets?'

...and the answer they get most often is 'communication'.

Organisational communication problems are endemic:

- Matrix organisations where project or operations managers don't tell line or functional managers how people are doing
- Businesses where all individual annual objectives are treated as secrets
- Virtual teams who never connect or gel with each other, despite all the technological help available
- Directors and senior team members who fail to consult their people and stakeholders about major change initiatives
- Managers who delay booking and then repeatedly cancel performance management meetings with their people
- Presenters who have clearly never listened to themselves
- Colleagues who sit within feet of each other and exchange emails but don't speak

- Meetings where decisions are not made and action plans not agreed
- Frontline staff who don't listen to customers
- Everybody writing and sending emails but not reading the emails they receive
- Everybody CCing everybody else into their emails, expecting them to find and action any points that apply to them
- 'Caller announce' telephones and voicemail being used to screen out and avoid people and messages
- 'Motivational' posters that nobody notices or reads
- 'Listeners' who are not listening, but rehearsing what they want to say in their heads while waiting for a gap so they can interrupt

In improv terms, these are all examples of blocking and denial: not listening to others, not accepting the reality of the situation we find ourselves in, looking to disagree first, seeing the people around us as obstacles, competitors or opponents rather than colleagues and stakeholders.

There is a proliferation of communication methods and technological solutions now at our disposal: face-to-face and one-to-one meetings, presentations, group discussions, telephones and voicemail, emails, memos and letters, noticeboards and posters, social media and online chat, texts and messaging. But they don't seem to have solved any of the problems. There are plenty of learning resources available to help workers address these issues and solve their communications problems. But the problems aren't going away. So maybe the learning resources aren't really helping either.

For many years, Harry and Julia designed and delivered learning interventions, including communication training courses, before they became interested in improv. They created and ran such programmes as Better Business Writing, Presentation Skills, Influencing, Effective Negotiation, and Managing and Handling Conflict. They knew that in many ways these were typical of the kind of learning interventions that organisations ran to improve communication, and commonly based on an underlying cyclical model of good behaviour at work: Plan, Do, Review – with the emphasis on 'plan'. Their programmes had face validity – they looked and felt useful – and got decent evaluations. But they seemed to be missing something: many learners did not appear to engage deeply with the issues or problems during programmes, or take away and act upon the learning once they returned to their day jobs.

Harry's best example of this is a group of learners who claimed, on the morning of the second day of a management development event, to have forgotten the entire content of the previous day's work because they'd 'slept since then'.

In addition, organisational learning and development functions tend to ignore listening and receptive communication. There seem to be a number of reasons for this:

- It's unglamorous, unshowy and easily forgotten or passed over.
- It's an internalised, convergent process.
- It's often associated with submissive and passive behaviour.
- It's often done well by more introverted people.

So while there's a lot of good in conventional learning and development interventions and programmes (they're not 'broken'), they could be a lot better.

How can improv help?

Improv workshops and programmes seemed similar to a lot of business training at first glance, but as Harry and Julia explored them further, they began to seem strikingly different.

Yes: improv scenes in workshops were all about people communicating, to each other and to their audience of other workshop participants. They were often funny and surprisingly insightful about people and life in general. Participants in improv scenes were obviously 'acting', and therefore not being real, but were clearly not following plans or working from scripts – real or imaginary – and could sometimes behave in ways that looked and felt authentic and honest. And the learning (about improv, but also about communication in general) seemed to get into their heads, sticking and niggling at them, in ways that more conventional organisational training courses just didn't.

Why was this? Harry and Julia think there are a number of reasons, the first being most important:

The brief given to improv workshop participants is distinctly different to that given to most learners on conventional communications training. The strongest positive instruction is 'listen'. This puts the emphasis clearly on receptive rather than expressive communication. This is unlike most organisational communication training. When was the last time you attended a programme or event called Better Business Reading, Listening Skills, or How to be Influenced?

Improv training is about practice. There's not much theory and it's not difficult to comprehend. But you need to do it a lot to really embed it into your behaviour. And once it's there, helping you to do improv, it's also available to you in other circumstances and situations.

The tasks that learners undertake in improv workshops are fun, engaging and impossible to do wrong. Humour seems to engage with people's creativity. The level of engagement involves conscious and unconscious thinking as well as the emotions and bodies of the learners who become completely immersed in the tasks.

Improv has surprising links to 'deeper' ideologies, philosophies and beliefs. In Bricolage (an important improv term, meaning both DIY and creating from what is at hand) it has similarities to the core Buddhist idea that 'everything you need is already inside you/around you'. Improv has been likened to meditation, as it can deliver a kind of grounded, centred, present mindfulness, but in a highly stimulating environment.

There's a whole undiscovered country out there of exercises, games and scenes that deliver on listening-related learning objectives, and are built on a wealth of experience, practice and theory in the training and development of actors and improvisers.

We are going to cover the following areas:

- Exercises for every day or team meetings
- Workshop exercises
- Listening exercises you can do by yourself

Exercises for every day or team meetings

You can introduce these exercises to your regular team meetings, or try them out with a group of willing colleagues.

Repeat before you reply

This is a two-person conversation, which can be about anything: this workshop, what you did last night, or where you plan to go on holiday. They have a normal conversation. BUT before either person can reply, they must repeat the other person's previous line EXACTLY.

This is simple to explain and run, but surprisingly hard to do. People are not used to immediately repeating what they hear, and because they don't have to, they don't do it well. In running this exercise it's important to police the participants: they must exactly repeat what they hear before they can say anything on their own behalf. If numbers permit, you can run this in trios, with one person being the observer/policewoman.

This exercise forces participants to listen to the entire content of their colleague's message, to internalise it and reproduce it before they can compose and say what they want. It stops them 'denying the other person's reality' and makes them engage with the conversation. There's an interesting bandwidth thing going on here. If we are really listening to the people around us, we don't have the mental processing power to simultaneously create and rehearse our own message.

Repeatedly practising this exercise trains people to do one thing at a time. Listen, then think, then speak. It's very useful as a precursor to the kind of coaching and feedback skills needed by managers during performance management appraisals, without appearing to be too 'psychological'.

Elevator pitch, or Cocktail party chat

It's important to be able to communicate clearly to others what you're doing and why you're doing it. For example, when your CEO follows you into the lift at work and says 'What are you working on at the moment?', and you only have the time it takes for the lift to reach the desired floor to make an impression.

Practise in teams, departments, job families or other groups, answering such questions as 'What are you working on at the moment?', and 'What's your department/function/team/organisation for?'

The point of this practice is NOT to develop a script or plan. Rather, it's about listening to your own and everyone else's approach and reflecting on what the rules of narrative are for short simple stories in business settings.

Remember:

- No planning in advance.
- Listen to yourself and others non-judgementally.
- Repeat, but don't look for incremental or organic improvement – that would mean you were developing a script. Try to keep it different every time.

Presentation skills programmes and events tend to concentrate on planning and preparation, expressive skills. This exercise is different: it de-emphasises the talking and puts the focus on listening and being in the moment.

Workshop exercises on listening

When you have more time, on an away day or during a workshop, you can use the following more advanced exercises that introduce the idea of playing and not being yourself.

Observation repeat conversation

This is an odd little exercise that is surprisingly powerful.

Two people have a conversation. The first person makes an observation about their partner. The second person repeats the observation (changing 'you' for 'I', etc.). The first repeats it again.

They go on repeating it, while they explore what it means, and what additional meaning can be brought to it through changes in their approach, or style of saying it. When the phrase is thoroughly worn out, the second person makes a new observation and the process goes round again. It repeats as long as the participants get something out of it.

Actors can use this exercise to focus their attention on the fine details of their fellow actors, or to explore the different ways a simple phrase can be said or interpreted. But as a work communication exercise it is more useful to think of it as internal exploration. What do the words mean, in context, to the participants? How much are they listening to their partners or rehearsing a new approach in their heads?

Customer service

Two people leave the room. While they are out of earshot, another person becomes the customer service employee and the rest of the participants decide what 'faulty purchase' is going to be returned to the customer service department of a large shop.

The wanderers return and have to present and complain about their purchase, without knowing what it is. They may say something like 'We plugged it in and put it on the kitchen work surface but it didn't work', then listen very carefully to how the customer service employee responds. They have to guess what they are complaining about.

At first the customer service employee is unhelpful and very straight, pointing out where suggestions are very silly or inappropriate. As time goes on they start to give more explicit clues about what the purchase is. Much hilarity ensues.

This exercise is all about listening. Picking up all the cues and clues from the customer service employee and the audience that suggest what the faulty item is. Staying curious, even when you're confused. Getting used to being in a state of not knowing, of finding out. Getting used to sticking to your guns even when people are laughing at you, not with you. Certainty is not a given in the modern workplace: curiosity, probing and listening skills are all competencies needed nowadays.

Loud business meeting

The participants are two colleagues having a serious and not at all exciting one-to-one business meeting. Not their first: they already know each other and don't need to cover the niceties or stay on best behaviour.

Each believes that the other is partially deaf and/or dense, dumb, dim, dopey, dull and doltish. They are too polite to actually talk about this, or call the other on it. But they talk loudly at each other in short simple sentences. Not angrily, but possibly with a somewhat patronising tone.

That's it. It's very funny. But it has serious implications. The loudness and simplicity forces people to listen to themselves and to others. It forces messages to be straightforward, without nuance or subtext. As an energiser in the midst of a number of communication role-plays it can work wonders.

Limericks
Most people know how a limerick works:

Be duddily duddily dum
Be duddily duddily mum
Be duddily doo
Be duddily poo
Be duddily duddily bum

Five lines... The first, second and fifth all rhyme. The third and fourth rhyme with each other but not with the first, second and fifth.

The first two lines set up a story, like the verse of a song, or like the thesis in dialectical analysis. The next two present a different perspective, like the middle eight or bridge of a song, or the antithesis. The last line brings the original rhyme back, hopefully informed by all that's gone before in synthesis, and ideally delivering a punchline – rude, crude and lewd, ideally – on the last word.

For example, a limerick about 'My Boss':

He certainly gathers no moss
And never read Mill on the Floss
His reports are so harsh
With the tone of Jean Marsh

36

Work on Communication

But really I don't give a toss!

Limericks can seem hard when you write them by yourself, so they must be impossible to do in a group of five people, live, out loud and without planning, with each person taking a line.

No. Not really. Five people stand in a line facing the other people in the workshop. A simple subject matter is sought from the audience. Anything, really: hamsters or NATO or whatever. The first person steps forward and says 'This is a limerick about hamsters' (or NATO or whatever). They then immediately say the first line. It's a good idea to express a strong positive or negative opinion about the subject ('I love...' or 'I hate...').

The second person has a harder job, as they have to listen on two levels, to the content and to the rhyme. They have to immediately produce a line that continues the story and rhymes.

Person 3 is listening for the story, in order to progress it in a slightly new direction. They need to hear the rhyme only enough to not use it themselves.

The fourth person's got more work to do again, progressing the story and rhyming with person 3.

The last person in the line has the hardest job, but has the most time to do it in. They need to complete the story in a satisfying way, return to the original rhyme and ideally, make the last word at least suggestive if not downright disgusting.

Everybody – participants and audience – laugh. Applause is shared.

LISTEN! SAY YES! COMMIT!

After the limerick is finished, all the participants shuffle up and the person at one end runs round to the other end. And then they create another limerick, with everyone in a new role. Repeat until all participants have delivered all lines.

Of course, this is funny and embarrassing in roughly equal measures. But it's also an intense and engaging listening exercise. Nothing works unless all the participants listen to and support each other, and trust their unconscious language centres to deliver the in-between words linking the rhymes. Generating the rhyming words themselves takes up most of the mind's conscious bandwidth: you just have to trust yourself to unconsciously put them into a roughly sensible semantic and grammatical context.

As it's a team activity, it's good for reinforcing collaboration and group mind, which is based, of course, on listening.

Listening exercises you can do by yourself

So how do we train ourselves to listen more deeply when we're (working) by ourselves? Here are some ideas:

Writing and reading a diary

Writing a diary is good for you. Read '59 Seconds' by Professor Richard Wiseman (2009) for the psychological theory and evidence backing up this assertion. Writing a diary is also a great way to train your ear and eye, especially when you read it back to yourself, and even more especially when you read it aloud.

When you read your writing back to yourself out loud, maybe after you've stuck it in a drawer, or left it in an unopened Word file for a day or a week, a month or a year, you can really see what you're doing wrong. And right. Whatever.

Reading prose and poetry out loud

You could also choose your favourite literature, journalism and poetry and read it out loud. There are no hard and fast rules here, in terms of what you choose or how low long you read for, but good writing feels different when you have to get your mouth and ears round it rather than just your eyes. You'll notice new and different things. Most poetry is designed to be read out loud: reading it in your head is like only ever driving a Maserati at 30 mph.

Listen to recordings of yourself talking

You hate the sound of your own voice when you hear it, pre-recorded, coming out of a speaker. Everyone does. But you can really learn from it.

LISTEN! SAY YES! COMMIT!

These rules still apply:

- No planning in advance.
- Listen to yourself and others non-judgementally.
- Repeat, but don't look for incremental or organic improvement – that would mean you were developing a script. Try to keep it different every time.

Feature: Psychological flexibility

In psychology, this concept is defined as:

'The ability to contact the present moment, and all the thoughts and feelings it contains without needless defence, and based on what the situation affords' and 'To persist or change behaviour in the service of chosen values' (Hayes et al., 2006).

Here is the model:

Recent studies have shown that increasing psychological flexibility improves employee wellbeing (see Flaxman et al., 2013). Currently, the interventions used have not been improv-based, but improv practice appears to offer

41

LISTEN! SAY YES! COMMIT!

a method through which individuals can practise most of the elements that comprise psychological flexibility.

Chapter 3: SAY YES! Work on Creativity

Harry and Julia are asked about creativity a great deal by clients. Also about its cousin, innovation. Typical questions are: 'How can I get myself/my team/my department to be more creative?', or 'How do I encourage innovation?' and 'How do I support people to think differently in my company?'

So, let's consider some definitions in relation to the workplace.

Creativity
'The generation of ideas or products that are novel and appropriate' (Cooper and Argyris, 1998)

Innovation
'The creation and implementation of an idea' (Cooper and Argyris, 1998)

While businesses value creativity, they also need innovation. An idea without a home (i.e. an application) is just that, an idea. Research has shown that one of the key factors that influence the level of innovation in a work setting is the climate for innovation: how much being creative, generating ideas and trying new things is supported by others, and (perhaps more importantly) those in positions of authority. In this chapter we will give you tools and techniques to boost you and your colleagues' creativity in different situations.

Practising these on a regular basis will encourage a climate for innovation.

Truly original and inventive ideas are rare. What we are typically required to do at work is to come up with solutions to problems, or find new ways to complete a task, or more efficient ways to run a process. While there are some more obviously creative professions – composer, writer, musician – all jobs nowadays require an element of creativity, or more likely, innovation.

The human brain is a wonderfully adaptive piece of kit; it works on being quick and efficient at its tasks, and once it learns how to do something (e.g. driving a car) the neural pathway becomes set. We like to use the analogy of a herd of cows to represent this idea. If you've ever looked at a field where cows live, there will be well-worn paths across it. Every day when the herd is brought in, they use the same path; even if this path is now not the most direct route, they will follow it (and each other).

This is what happens in the brain: neural impulses follow the same pathways over and over again. It is now known that our brains retain the ability to adapt and to make new links (a concept called neuroplasticity) throughout adult life. But this will not happen without some proactive input; the relatively unexplored pathways will not be followed unless you do something different. In the case of cows, placing something in their way will make them create a new path to go around the obstacle. So to create new pathways in your brain, you need to find ways to actively direct your thoughts away from the well-trodden pathway.

But it is not enough just to say 'think differently'; your mind needs guidance to veer off the path and discover new routes which is why there are 'rules' in most improv exercises.

Paradoxically, creativity needs structure, something to push up against.

Before we move on, it is worth mentioning 'thinking on your feet', as this notion seems to be closely linked to creativity and innovation in most people's minds, and we are often asked to include this topic in our workshops. A definition we have found is 'to make a quick decision or give an answer quickly'.

The key here is the reference to speed. Everyone's idea of 'quickly' is likely to vary depending on what they're used to. It's about perception, because in reality we all think on our feet all the time; life is (for most of the time) improvised in that we haven't decided what to say before we open our mouths. When people say that they want to be better at thinking on their feet, what they actually seem to want to improve is their spontaneity. Or more accurately, their level of comfort when they are required to be spontaneous. We will talk about how to incorporate 'spontaneity training' into your plans in the next section.

How can improv help?

Creativity
We say 'yes' a lot in comedy improvisation. We are actively encouraged to say yes a great deal (sometimes literally), but always to say yes to what is offered: the situation, who you are, what day it is.

If someone says 'Hello officer, I was only doing about 30 miles an hour', then it is clear who you are supposed to be in the scene. If you respond by saying 'I'm not a police officer', if you block or deny the offer, then the scene is dead. You have rejected the offer and effectively said no. How much more pleasing if you respond: 'I am well aware of your speed, Mrs Jones – I just stopped you to tell you that I liked your blouse!' Now there's a scene I want to see more of!

Saying yes is very important to creativity. Saying no usually kills an idea, or at the very least slows it down. A common way to express this in improv circles is 'yes, and...' rather than 'yes, but...'. A great many workplaces spend a lot of time focusing on 'yes, but'. This is fine for critical evaluation, but not for being creative. For that you need 'yes, and'. Many exercises that we use in improvisation are great tools for improving your creativity.

Spontaneity

Your typical improviser, when pointed at out of the blue by someone else and told to 'name a breed of dog – quick as you can', will be inclined to think 'Oh good, a game to play!' and will blurt out 'whippet' or 'schnauzer' quick as a flash. A non-improviser will feel put on the spot and will be inclined to think 'Oh no, my mind has gone blank'. They often attempt to defer the request: 'Why? What's the point of that?' (Remember, a question always throws the responsibility back to the other person; questions are only useful when they add information.) Contrast with: 'Oh, give me a minute – while I'm thinking, you name a breed of cat'.

The only way to become more comfortable with spontaneity is to practise being spontaneous. Doing the exercises in this chapter (or this book for that matter) on a regular basis, on your own or with colleagues, will increase your comfort with being asked to do or say things on the spot.

Spontaneity and creativity are the two elements that characterise improvisation. At work, sometimes you need one or the other, sometimes both. We are going to focus on creativity, but remember, all these exercises will help you to gain comfort with being spontaneous.

The areas we are going to cover are:

- Warming up before a creative task
- Generating ideas 'from a blank sheet of paper'
- Redesigning or refining existing processes

Getting started: warm-up exercises

The warm-up exercises we suggest will help you to go off to different places in your brain more easily, and this will ultimately result in new links and pathways.

In our troupe we often do these exercises at the start of a rehearsal to get into a divergent way of thinking or open things up. Often the words and themes that come up during these sessions will crop up during our improvising later, an example of an effect known as priming.

Think about this in a work setting. A team meets to come up with an idea to solve a pressing problem. At the start of the meeting all that is talked about is the problem and how difficult it is going to be to deal with. This essentially primes everyone in the room to think about the issue in the same way and keeps everyone's focus myopic.

Instead, spend 5–10 minutes talking about other things, anything at all, the wider the subject matter the better. Even if you don't have the chance to do any of the structured warm-ups suggested below, just talk about what everyone did last night or at the weekend. Everyone's brains will have been down different paths, so when you come to discuss the 'problem' you will see it afresh.

Free association (with some structure)

You can do this on your own or in a group. In a group it is best if you stand in a circle. The first person starts with one word. If you need inspiration, look around the room or out of the window and name something you see, e.g. grass, and say the word out loud.

The next person repeats the word and then free associates with it, e.g. 'Grass – which makes me think of – green'.

The next person says: 'Green – which makes me think of – blue'.

Then: 'Blue – which makes me think of – Joni Mitchell'.

Keep going round the circle.

Important points to remember:

- Associate only with the previous word – that's why repeating the word and saying 'which makes me think of...' is important. Otherwise the words tend to form lists of related items, e.g. green – blue – yellow – red – letter – writing – post – stamp. Although this is fine, remember we are using this exercise to think as divergently as possible.
- There are no wrong answers – whatever the previous word makes you think of, say it!
- Keep going for as long as you like or until someone notices a link back to the starting word, e.g. skittle – bowling – lawn – grass. It's great if you succeed in this, but don't force it!

NB Another way to generate a starting word is to pick up a book and turn to any page, close your eyes and point.

Advanced version for a group: layering associations.

Standing in circle, one person steps into the centre and says: 'I am...' (any word, e.g. 'liberty').

Two other people then step forward to join the first and offer an association with the first word, e.g. 'I am freedom'; 'I am a London department store'.

The first person then chooses one of the associations (the one they like the best), and the chosen person remains in the circle and repeats the new starting word, e.g. 'I am London department store'. The others return to their places.

Two new people from the circle step forward as before to associate with the new word/concept, e.g. 'I am Harrods'; 'I am luxury'. Repeat for as long as you like.

Brain gym

This exercise is done in groups of four. It is an excellent way to wake your brain up and get everyone thinking about different things.

Choose a 'target' person. This is the person whose brain will be exercised (the most!). One person (B) stands opposite the target person and performs gentle physical movements (think Tai Chi) which the target person must mirror at all times during the exercise. So, if person B slowly raises their left arm above their head, the target person slowly raises their right arm above their head.

Another person (A) stands on the right side of the target person and asks them 'experiential' questions. By this, we mean questions that don't (usually) have right and wrong answers, and that ask about aspects of the person's life, such as: 'What's your favourite colour?', 'When did you last eat an ice-cream?', 'Football or rugby?'.

The final person (C) stands on the left side of the target person and asks them factual questions, e.g. 'What's the capital of Italy?'; 'What is two plus six?'; 'Who is the Prime Minister?'.

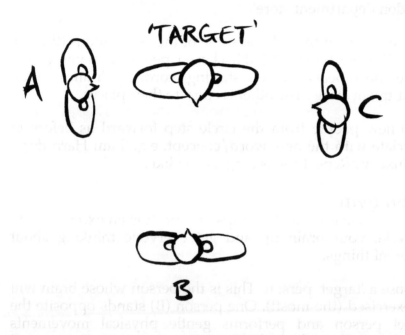

Once everyone has established their role you can start. The questioners must fire questions at the target person throughout: if they don't hear, repeat until they do. The target person must answer as many questions as they can. If they don't know the answer, they can say 'don't know', and for the experiential questions it is permitted to say 'I don't want to answer that' as required.

At the end of the time, rotate the roles. Repeat twice more so that everyone has performed every role. For a quick warm-up, do two minutes per rotation. For a real workout, do five minutes per rotation.

The idea is for the target person to feel slightly overloaded, as this exercise requires several different areas of the brain to be active in order to perform all the tasks. In practice, the questioners also tend to find the act of generating the questions quite challenging and a brain warm-up in itself!

Learning to accept the feeling of being overloaded – having more to do or think about than you can handle consciously and deliberately – is important for improv, and for authenticity, which we'll talk about in more detail in Chapter 5. A lot of the improv exercises described in this book are intended to tie up the conscious mind in arbitrary rules and abstract behaviour in order to allow unconscious speech and behaviour (normally censored and constrained) to come out. If we set goals about how we want to think, act or talk, and practise unplanned behaviour while uncritically watching and listening to what we do, we can watch our unconscious behaviour move slowly toward our goals.

Point and name
This is a classic improv warm-up that encourages both creativity and spontaneity.

If space allows, have everyone mill around the room freely. Try not to get into a pattern. If you notice that everyone is moving around in a circle, change direction. The movement helps with the thinking.

Now, everyone separately and repeatedly points at different objects in the room and says the name of each object out loud. Try to just point without identifying the object first – then just name what you see:

'Basket – poster – beam – collecting tin – brass plate – wall – green book – wheelchair...'

As I am writing this in a situation where I can't shout out random words, I just did the exercise in my head. So if you are doing this exercise on your own in a setting that doesn't allow you to shout the words out (on the Tube, in a library or coffee shop) then you can do it silently.

Make sure everyone is pointing definitely and saying the words confidently. Now change it up. This time when you point at an object you must say what it is not – anything at all except what it actually is:

'Fruit – rollover – France – Wellington boot – frying pan – West Pier...'. Say anything. It doesn't matter if it comes out as 'thingummy' or 'bleugh' sometimes. Try not to get into patterns even though your brain will try to do that for you, e.g. all fruit, or days of the week.

This exercise helps to get you into thinking differently. It's also slightly silly, which is good too. Pointing at your colleague and shouting 'weathervane' certainly builds rapport in a rather different way than usual!

Rolodexing
This helps to broaden vocabulary and concept usage.

There are two types of Rolodex exercise.

Work on Creativity

The first is generating simple lists of objects in a given category. Each person lists ten objects in the category provided by the person next to them, e.g. ten types of car, ten things you might find on the beach, ten brands of toothpaste.

While the person is naming ten things, the others count steadily from one to ten. They do not wait for the person to list an object before counting. This is important because it means that the 'lister' doesn't get stuck because the group is waiting. Most of the time, this means that the person doesn't end up listing ten things. This doesn't matter, but they should always attempt to list ten things.

The second kind of Rolodex exercise is where the first person names an object and then each person in the circle takes turns to name a list that that object could appear on. For example, the object could be 'a magazine'. Person 1 might say 'a list of items you can buy in the newsagents'. Person 2 says 'articles made of paper'. Person 3 says 'things you might find on my coffee table at home'; the next person, 'words that begin with m'.

Continue around the circle until the person who said 'magazine' has named a list. Then the next person names a new object for everyone to create a list for.

Sometimes it takes people a while to grasp this exercise, but persevere, as it is a great way to broaden your thinking. Once you have done this with random words you could do a version specific to the task to lead into your ideas generation. For example, if your session is concerned with generating ideas for a new financial services product (such as a pension), you could use related lists: things associated with old age, types of allowance, things you can collect at the post office, things that people put off organising, benefits provided by employers, things people wish were bigger (now there's an interesting list!).

Generating ideas: exploration (blank sheet of paper stuff)

'Creativity in organisations is associated with uncertainty, ambiguity, conflict and risk' (West and Markiewicz, 2004)

Some tasks at work are more obviously creative than others: coming up with the name for a new service, writing an advertising strapline, inventing a new product. It's obvious that you're going to need to be creative, and your workplace is most likely to be supportive of using creative approaches. This section focuses on techniques that can help you in situations where you are starting with nothing, and have to come up with something.

Structured brainstorming

Research has shown that classic brainstorming, while generating buy-in from the participants, isn't usually very successful at generating workable new ideas.

Most unstructured sessions I have seen go something like this:

Whoever is in charge writes up 'the problem' on a flip chart and then says 'any ideas?', or they say 'I was thinking x, y, z – everyone agree?'. Either way, the group gets into discussing what is good about the initial ideas before spending a proper amount of time generating as many as possible.

For effective brainstorming, it is essential that you set aside a decent period of time where there is no censoring of ideas at all and everyone gets a chance to input. If you fear that some members of the group will feel inhibited then do some of this individually, where people write on post-its and stick them up. There is some evidence that individuals come up with better ideas on their own, but to benefit from the combined effort and skills of everyone, use both individual and group ideas.

Before you start, make sure that you have a clear statement of intent concerning the outcome of the session, such as:

'By the end of this session, we will have a shortlist of five possible names for our new xx service.'

Or:

'By the end of this session, we will have agreed on a slogan for the xx advertising campaign.'

Now use several of the following exercises to open up your thinking about the topic.

Remember the rules:

- There are no right and wrong answers.
- Everyone's contribution is equal.
- All ideas are good ideas – do not criticise anyone's suggestions.

Yes, and...

Again, this could be about a random topic or one relevant to the team. For example:

'It's our team away day next month, and I'd really like us to go to Blackpool.'

'Yes, and we could all go up Blackpool Tower together.'

'Yes, and we could have a dancing lesson in the Tower Ballroom.'

'Yes, and we could eat fish and chips on the beach.'

'Yes, and Len Goodman could come with us.'

'Yes, and...'

Analogies

'If the service/product was a type of car, bird, pudding, fashion designer, animal, what would it be?'

This can be done individually or as a group. Capture the output as it is: remember the rules.

Word association on the topic

If you are developing an advertising slogan or campaign or product name, this is a good way to open up your thinking.

Take a word that is related to your product/service e.g. 'innovation' and free associate with it. Use the same method as in the warm-up exercise, or just shout out. Write up everything everyone says – however crazy it seems!

Lists

Ten things people say about our new product/service

Ten things people don't say about our new product/service

Work in the present tense, as if the product or service already exists, e.g. 'This is the best thing since sliced bread' or 'This nail varnish has improved my confidence at work'.

Sentence completion

This works well if you imagine the end customer. If you have a clear segmentation of customers, you could allocate different people in the group to each. This is a good exercise to do individually.

'I picked it up in the shop because...'

'Someone recommended this to me because...'

'I really liked it because...'

'What was brilliant about the service was...'

'The best thing about the product is...'

'I would really like to tell the company that made this that...'

Interviews and conversations

Carry out a mock interview, with one person playing the company spokesperson and one playing a journalist from the trade press. The interview is taking place at the product/service launch.

Get into pairs and have a conversation between two customers about the new product/service. Be two customers who are huge fans of the new product/service, then two who hate it, and then one of each.

Capture key phrases that the 'customers' say. If numbers allow, you could work in trios and have an observer who does this. If you wanted to, you could play Customer Service, the exercise described in the previous chapter.

During ideas generation, try to build on others' ideas by thinking 'yes, and'. As mentioned earlier, this phrase crops

57

up a great deal in improv and you may have come across it before. It really helps. At this stage, anything is possible, resources are limitless, and craziness is encouraged. 'Yes, but' is banned entirely from this stage of brainstorming!

If you are in a group of more than two or three, then it's best if you write all your ideas up on flipcharts and post them round the room so that everyone can see them easily. With two or three of you, you might manage with large sheets of paper on the table.

We created the ideas for our book using many of these methods. On the way, we talked about many entirely unrelated topics as they occurred to us. We never worried about this, as talking about all the 'and that makes me think of' themes sparks new ideas. During our sessions we jotted down the things we talked about and then afterwards we used a word cloud app to capture everything and provide a visual record to refer back to.

Never worry about what you are producing or the apparent quality of it. This is a divergent process; much of what is produced will never be used directly, but it is creating new links in your head all the time. The one golden nugget produced from an all-day structured brainstorming may look as if it came from nowhere, but it was more than likely a product of what came before it, even if the link is not bivouac (don't you just love spell check – I wanted to type 'obvious'). That golden nugget could make your company thousands or millions of pounds – you can't expect to jump straight to it.

Refinement
The next stage of structured brainstorming is to start refining the ideas you have generated. At this point, you might just have a room full of flipcharts covered in seemingly random

words. Don't worry! Get everyone to walk around the room and look at everything. Then take a break.

Studies have shown that stopping thinking about a problem for a while helps with finding a solution. It is even better if you also perform a repetitive, unrelated task. Drinking tea will do, or you could walk round the block.

Now you get everyone to walk around the room again, look at the flipcharts and start noting down the ideas that come to them. This could be suggestions for the service/product name, draft ad straplines or product outlines. Then put these up on another flipchart and review.

At this point you can begin to read the ideas that you have on a scale for feasibility. But try not to dismiss ideas that any one person likes out of hand without first exploring whether these could be possibilities. At this stage you are beginning the process of converging on a solution. Aim to get as close as possible to achieving the objective that you set at the start of the session.

At whatever point you finish, make sure you assign someone to capture your output in a way that it can be accessed again. This used to involve some poor soul typing up all the flipcharts, but nowadays we tend to take photos of them and then drop these into a document that can be circulated. It is also recommended that next steps are clearly outlined, otherwise all your efforts at creativity will disappear into the ether. There is a reason why writers, artists and other creatives always carry a notebook or voice recorder – sparks of genius are elusive, drifting up from the subconscious when we least expect them. Capturing those thoughts in some way is very important.

LISTEN! SAY YES! COMMIT!

Once you have shortlist of feasible ideas to take forward, you need to move to a more practical and objective stage in your process to create a plan to implement one or more of them. If you get stuck at any point where further ideas seem necessary, flip back into creativity mode and carry out a mini version of the development session described above as required.

Feature: Improvisation and Divergent Thinking

Researchers at the University of Hertfordshire (Lewis and Lovatt, 2013) have carried out studies that provide some evidence for the link between improv practice and subsequent improvements in divergent thinking. Participants in the experiment were assigned to two groups – those who carried out improv exercises, and a control group who carried out similar but not improvisational tasks.

The researchers found that the group who practised improv improved their scores on a divergent thinking task significantly more than the control group in terms of fluency, originality and flexibility of their ideas. They explain their results in relation to schema theory.

Schemas are general knowledge structures that we build up subconsciously throughout life to make sense of our knowledge of the world. In our daily lives we employ schemas to deal with the situations that we encounter, such as using pre-planned script phrases in commonly encountered scenarios, for example the teacher who repeats the same phrase whenever the class is noisy! Lewis and Lovatt propose that actively engaging in improvisational exercises helps people to stimulate under-used neural pathways, encouraging them to break out of their set patterns of thought and move away from convergent thinking to come up with new ideas. Although this study is relatively exploratory it does show how practising improvisation exercises can influence creativity.

Process redesign: working with what you have – Bricolage

Where the boundaries are more tightly set and you can only work with what you've got, you have to be more focused. Examples of this might be where you have to reduce the length of a process by a certain number of days or hours, or you have to save x% costs for a project.

Bricolage (French for tinkering) is defined as the construction or creation of a work from a diverse range of things that happen to be available, or a work created by such a process. Academics also refer to 'psychological bricolage' or 'creative cognition' which is conceptualised as the cognitive processes that enable individuals to retrieve and recombine previously unrelated knowledge they already possess. This has been proposed as being an essential skill for 21st-century organisations to possess (see Weick, 1998).

As mentioned before, creativity welcomes structure. Although it might at first seem constraining, the boundaries are set, your ballpark is defined, so you have a safe space in which to play.

Of course, you may be able to rework your process in a straightforward way; it could be obvious that the reason payroll is late every fourth month is because the employee responsible for signing off the final roll doesn't work on a Friday. But even that may not be obvious until you spend some time breaking the process apart or interrogating it thoroughly. The following exercises are aimed at helping you and your team to look at the process or project in some new and different ways to facilitate bricolage.

Machines

As an improv exercise, this is about creating fantastical machines from audience suggestions, so notable examples might be the 'Christmas machine', the 'jealousy machine' and the 'failed romance machine'. But you can use this exercise for a much more practical purpose.

Imagine your process is one machine. Four or five people are going to act out this machine using themselves to represent aspects of the machine. The first person starts with one idea which they repeat, then a second person joins them as the next 'cog' doing something else that complements the first, then the next person, then the next, until everyone has joined and the whole machine runs for three iterations. You can use physicality (position and/or movement) as well as sounds, words or noises. Let's imagine that the process is a recruitment process for graduate trainees.

First person standing makes a movement as if proffering a piece of paper, and says 'Fill it in!' in a stern-sounding voice. They should leave a gap before repeating the movement and the phrase to allow space for the other participants to join.

Second person kneels next to the first person with one hand grasping their leg, and makes a crying noise whilst rubbing their eyes with the other hand.

Third person stands behind the first person with a hand on the first person's shoulder. Immediately after the first person says 'Fill it in!', they pop their head around the side of the first person and say 'Computer says no' in a cheerful voice, then return to their initial position.

Fourth person lies down across the front of the 'machine' and makes a noise as if being crushed by a great weight.

So the final auditory sequence goes: Fill it in, Computer says no, Boo-hoo, Aaarrrgh!

A couple of guidelines for Machines are that each person who joins should be in physical contact with the existing machine in some way. This is to convey the idea that the machine is one entity. Each participant that joins should try to fit into what is there already, find the gaps in the process. Whatever occurs to you is right!

So what can you do with the output of this? Well, the recruitment process machine described suggests that the process is attracting a lot of candidates (creaking under the weight) but seems to be rejecting a lot of candidates. The tone of the 'fill it in' request and the computer element suggests that it might be an impersonal process. Of course, the people involved in the process may have had an inkling that these aspects might be the problem already, but seeing it brought to life focuses the attention. You might then want to repeat the exercise, but creating a machine for the perfect recruitment process... What are the key differences?

Physical layout of the process in the room

Similar to the game Machines above, in that you use people to represent the elements of a process, you lay this game out in the room using the space to represent time or location aspects of the process. It is helpful to have a director for this exercise. They place the people how they want them whilst telling them what they are.

Work on Creativity

So in our recruitment example:

Person A stands in the corner facing the wall to represent the online application process.

Person B stands in the middle of the room to represent the paper screening process.

Person C stands next to them to represent the emails sent to candidates accepting or rejecting them.

Person D sits in the opposite corner of the room with their arms out representing the hiring manager.

In this case, the gap between the computer and the paper screening might represent time: the computer is fast, but the paper screen is slow, so there is a blockage. Or it could represent the strength of the link: the computer is perceived as far away from the next part of the process and not visible (confirmed by the facing away).

Carrying out this sort of exercise taps into unconscious beliefs about the process and makes them visible to all. You might want to repeat this a few times with different directors to highlight the different mental models that people have of the process. Again, this can highlight where the problems might be in the process, so you can focus on areas that need work.

Another way to get into thinking about a process in a different way is to play some word games. It helps if you are able to be entirely irreverent about it. As someone once said, there's many a true word spoken in jest!

Metaphors

'If this process was an animal (make of car, sports team, vegetable) what would it be?'

Version 1: choose an appropriate animal with an obvious justification, e.g. this recruitment process is like an elephant – it's big and slow-moving.

Version 2: one person chooses a random animal, then another person justifies it, e.g. this recruitment process is like a hyena. Why? It looks ugly and it makes a hell of a noise!

Then you can try to expand the metaphors. How else is the process like an elephant? Never forgets anything? Has big ears (in a metaphorical sense)? Moves in herds?

As with structured brainstorming, play the game for a while without censoring so you allow your unconscious the time to throw out ideas. Find a way to capture the output in some way, then after a period of time you can have a look back at it and review it with your serious hat on:

What are the themes of your metaphors?

What surprised you, and what does that reveal about the current process?

What was not surprising and what does that confirm about the current process?

If it's bad make it worse!
This is a kind of reverse brainstorming. Ask yourselves:

- What could we do to make this process worse than it is already?
- If performance is currently 6/10 how could we make it 2/10, or even 1/10?
- What would be a sure way to not hit your targets?

Generate as many ideas as you can think of to crash the performance of your process. Making it worse, paradoxically can unlock a new or different way to make it better – it's also strangely cathartic! Once you have a list, try turning round your ideas to produce potential ways to improve the process.

Using the output from these exercises, you can then create a plan to take the ideas forward.

LISTEN! SAY YES! COMMIT!

Chapter 4: COMMIT! Work on Teamworking

Most people work in teams these days. And increasingly, these teams are not the static, all-sit-together-in-the-same-office type of teams, but project teams brought together for a particular piece of work, virtual teams who work in several locations and time zones, or a temporary group of individuals tasked with tackling an organisational issue or problem.

According to Professor Michael West of Lancaster University, you can tell if someone is in the same team as you if 'your work output is dependent on their work output to a significant extent'. Sometimes this is true, but you are not designated as a team – say, an informal team – making it even more difficult to work together effectively.

Research shows that teams need the following characteristics to work together effectively:

Purpose – clearly defined goals that are inspiring, challenging and important, and outcomes that are clear and measurable

Delegated responsibility – for achieving their goals

Manageable size – not fewer than three or more than 15 members

Clear identity – usually derived from the team's task

Diversity – enough differences between members to produce innovation, but not so much that there are constant arguments

Establishing these is difficult if you never see each other, or if you are only working on the same thing for a few weeks. Yet you are expected to perform as a unit, for example negotiations together, presentations, meetings to agree a business case. In addition, work teams tend to be relatively fluid these days, with people leaving and joining on a regular basis. This adds to the difficulties of maintaining the team.

A note about team size

The most effective teams are rarely larger than about 15 people, ideally 8 to 10. There are only so many people that you can maintain a decent relationship with at once, and that has been found to be about the same size as a typical extended family. In evolutionary terms we are lagging behind ourselves, so our ideal conditions as a species are still the same as they were several thousand years ago. If you think that you belong to a team that is larger than 16, then one of two things is going on. Either it is not actually a team (review whether everyone's work outputs are actually dependent on each other's), or it shouldn't be, and some reorganisation is in order, perhaps the creation of sub-teams.

How can improv help?

The very reason that Harry and Julia started introducing improv into their work was because of their observations in relation to teamworking and improv.

When you improvise with others you have to work together – we've already talked about accepting the offer made by a colleague in Chapter 3. Not only do you need to accept what is offered, and build on it, but you also need to do so with commitment. You do your best neither to block nor deny the reality of the situation or scene you are being offered. Your job as a team member in an improv setting is to make the other participant look good.

This is the antithesis of what happens in many workplaces, where competition and one-upmanship are rife. Every man and woman for themselves. Of course, you can do that in an improv scene – if you're funny, you will probably get some laughs. But after a while, your jokes will appear lame, your attempts to hog the scene and to look better than your partner will start to pall, and no one will want to play with you!

Improvisation is about 'holding on and letting go': it's about committing to the scene (to the team and the job or task you are undertaking right now), to your scene partners, fellow improvisers and colleagues, to supporting the ideas, actions and behaviours that are current. But it's also dropping the old as soon as it's no longer useful: dropping your own ideas if others get there first or are better, not worrying about the last thing you did in favour of focusing on what you are doing now, dropping your previous (default, go-to) relationships or characters when presented with the chance to work with new ones... Improvisers can look fickle or flighty, but the best improvisers are all 'early adopters'.

And improvisers trust each other. On the whole, it is not a solo activity, so you quickly learn that your success is dependent on the other participants. There is evidence that levels of trust in work groups can affect performance, job satisfaction, and levels of commitment, so finding a way to build trust is very important.

The other reason that improv creates trust in a group is because laughter brings people together as a group by signalling 'bonding, affirmation, belonging, listening'. You may find that many of the exercises we suggest in this chapter seem quite childish, and initially that may feel strange in a work setting. But persevere; as long as you create a safe environment for this with clear ground rules, team members will soon relish the joy and freedom afforded them by using these exercises.

None of this means that improv is necessarily easy, at least at first. Opening up to collaboration, to an ever-changing mix of new ideas, to dropping your own prepared position in favour of something that someone else only just thought of, to exposing some pretty revealing thoughts or opinions or actions... these can all be threatening. And in the face of threat and the negative feelings it brings with it, we may sabotage our improv experience or learning, like the teenager who 'accidentally' smashes a glass every time they are asked to wash the dishes, to prove that they are so bad at it that they should never be asked again. Some people get so used to sabotaging stuff that they even start to do it during activities they choose. That's when they become expert blockers, expressing positive ('I want to be here') and negative ('Don't talk to me. I'm bored and tired and I don't care') feelings simultaneously.

In teams, you can expect a wide variety of reactions to the ideas and practices of improvisation, so in this chapter we are going to cover a range of exercises that will help you and your team to work more effectively:

* Warm-ups that can be used in most team situations to create a team connection
* Activities for away days or team development workshops to build trust, group cohesion and involvement

Work on Teamworking

- Exercises for every day/team meetings to promote group working
- Ways to promote connection in virtual teams

Feature: Effectiveness of improv training at work

A quick Internet search reveals that there are many people (improvisers, management consultants, academics) using improv as the basis for interventions in organisations. What is less clear is how effective these interventions are (beyond the testimonials of satisfied clients!).

Does it make any difference to train employees or teams of employees in improv techniques? It is important to remember that in improv, the players use the process of improvising to create a performance, and this performance is also the output. In organisations, this is not generally the case. Here, the process of improvising can be employed to work towards a particular output (new product idea, strategy or whatever) but it is separate from it. Improv in organisations is just a process, and its outputs can be negative as well as positive.

Vera and Crossan (2005), were able to carry out a large study with 50 work teams (348 individuals) within a large US organisation. They assigned half the teams to receive improvisation-based training and collected data pre- and post-training concerning levels of collective improvisation and of innovation within the team. While they hypothesised that training in improvisation would lead to increases in the level of innovation, they also realised that it was unlikely to be as simple as that, and also proposed several moderating factors, as shown in the diagram below.

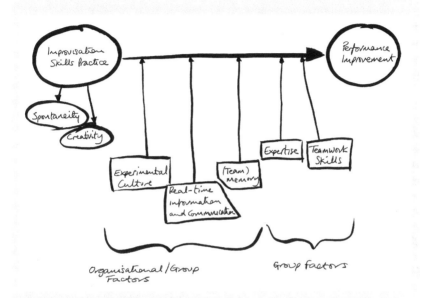

Overall, the results supported most of their hypotheses, with all but one of the proposed variables (memory) showing a positive moderating effect on the link between improvisation and innovation. The authors summarised their findings by saying 'improvisation is on average valueless, but has a clear positive effect on innovation when combined with team and contextual moderating factors'.

In other words, improv training works for teams when they already have the expertise and know-how to work together reasonably well, and when the company they work for supports them in their efforts to be innovative and provides decent information and communication.

These findings have since been supported by a study carried out in South Africa as part of a Masters degree thesis (Kirsten, 2008).

This study showed a significant improvement in the climate for work group innovation in a healthcare management team that had received improvisation training, as against a comparable control team that had not.

Overall, there is beginning to be some evidence for the efficacy of improv training, but it is also clear that certain conditions need to be in place if that training is to impact performance.

Warm-ups to be used in most team situations

When you meet as a team, it is a good idea to spend the first few minutes creating a connection between you as a group and starting to build an identity as a team. This is essential if you do not meet face-to-face as a team very often.

Share your stuff
This is not improv as such but is something most creative groups and companies use.

At the start of your team meetings take one minute each (timed) to share something with the team. Depending on your work environment, this could be about work, or personal life if that is appropriate. Agree the parameters that suit your team upfront. (If we feel we need a physical boost, then we do this whilst hopping on one foot!)

Work on Teamworking

As you grow more comfortable as a team, you can use this session to 'off-load' the negativity of the day or week. Having a good moan about the parking situation or the lack of Bounty bars in the vending machine helps to set it aside before the session proper begins!

The following exercises are best done standing in a circle (but don't have to be, as long as everyone can make eye contact with everyone else). All of these involve making eye contact with each other and require you to direct your full attention to your teammates.

Pass the clap (or click)
As it says, pass a clap round the circle one at a time.

Start by going round clockwise from person to person.

The first person claps at the same time as looking and gesturing at the target person.

As soon as you 'receive' the clap, pass it on to the next person. Once you are going, speed up and pass it on as quickly as possible (whilst retaining the eye contact).

Next, add in the possibility of changing direction whenever someone wants to. If that goes OK, the next level is to pass the clap to anyone at all in the circle at any time. This means that everyone must pay attention at all times to be ready to receive the clap and pass it on.

NB If clapping is too loud or obvious, you can use a finger click instead.

Sevens

A variant of passing a clap is to use groups of seven. This is a great warm-up as it incorporates word sequences as well as physical movements and focused attention.

Start with the numbers one to seven.

The first person says 'one' whilst using their left or right arm to slap their opposite shoulder (gently!). Using their left or right arm indicates the direction of their pass: left arm to right shoulder indicates to the right, and right arm to left shoulder to the left.

Start by going in one direction only to establish the pattern.

The second person says 'two', the third 'three', and so on until 'seven' which has a special arm movement: one arm is placed above and round the head, whilst at the same time, the other arm is placed across the body at waist height. This sort of creates an 'S' shape. Again, the arms can be placed either way, and the top arm indicates the direction of the pass.

After 'seven' has been said, the sequence starts again. This may sound simple, but the combination of physical movement, following the direction, and the sequence is challenging for most people. Speed up as you get more comfortable with it.

Now repeat the same pattern with another set of sevens – the days of the week, Monday to Sunday. Again, the direction can change at any time, and the seventh word has the special physical action to go with it. Do that for a while. Then mix up the two sets of seven, so at any point anyone can swap to the other.

The sequence might go like this:

One – two – Wednesday – four – Friday – Saturday – seven

Or:

Monday – two – three – four – Friday – six – Sunday

Remember to keep the physical moves going at the same time.

Up to this point, and if the exercise is new to people, if someone makes a mistake, just restart. But once your team feels more comfortable, you can introduce a 'forfeit' if someone messes up, for example by saying the wrong word, missing their turn or not using the special physical symbol for seven/Sunday. We often use walking round the outside of the circle, but if space or physical constraint does not allow for this, the person could just step back and count to 10. It is a good idea for each person to impose their own forfeit so they take responsibility for their own performance. At a very basic level, this is also good practice at acknowledging one's own mistakes.

Now you can add in another set of sevens – the first seven letters of the alphabet, A to G; the first seven months of the year, January to September. You can have all of these in use at the same time. Remember that the last in the sequence of seven always has the special S-shaped physical position.

Pattern games

This involves setting up web-like patterns amongst the team members and involves connection, memory and reaction time.

The first pattern uses the word 'you'. Say there are six people in your group. Person A points at person C and says out loud and decisively, 'you', then person C points at person D and says 'you', D points at F, F points at B, B to E, then E back to A. Each person has pointed at one other person until everyone has been pointed at and it gets back to the first person.

You now have a web pattern for the group (see example diagram below). For the first time round, keep your arms raised so it is clear who is left. Then repeat the pattern several times so you commit it to memory.

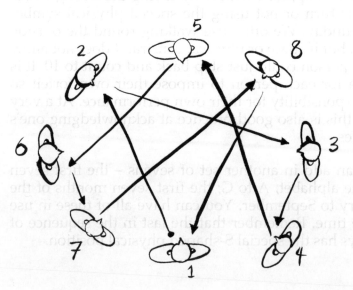

Work on Teamworking

Next, set up another entirely different pattern. This time, get a different person to start the pattern and use group members' names. For example, Wendy starts and points to Jane, who points to David, who points to Greg, who points to Katie who points at James who points back to Wendy. Each person should say the name of the person they are pointing at clearly and decisively. Again, keep arms up as you point the first time, then repeat the pattern until you have remembered it. It is a good idea to try to avoid pointing at the same person as you did in the last sequence, although this isn't always possible, depending on the size of the group.

Now you can try to get both patterns going at the same time. Start with 'you' then once that's established, add in the name pattern. Depending on where you are in each sequence, you might receive two 'points' at the same time. Try to pass on each as quickly as possible. The person pointing is responsible for making sure that their 'point' is received. Eye contact is really important here. As you become more confident with the patterns, you can drop the actual pointing and just use the word plus facial expression, eye contact and perhaps a head nod to indicate that you are passing.

Stop again whilst you establish a third pattern. This time use words in a category, such as fruit, colours or drinks. Again, set it up on its own with raised arms until everyone remembers it.

Try to get all three patterns going at the same time. If one drops out (which often happens), then start it up again.

If you can achieve three patterns at a time, then you are doing brilliantly and can attempt the next level which is to run all three patterns while changing places during the name pattern. So, as Wendy says 'Jane', she moves to stand where Jane is standing in the circle; Jane must quickly say, 'David' and start to move to his position in the circle, and so on. This is really difficult as all the physical location cues are messed up, so if you previously received 'you' from the left and passed it to the right, that won't be the case anymore. Aargh!

Walk-stop-jump
A great warm-up for beginning to develop 'group mind'.

Have the team mill around the room in no particular pattern without talking. The aim of the exercise is for everyone to stop and stand still at the same moment. Although this may seem an impossible aim when you first try it, it is achievable with practice.

Give instructions to the team members that they should not attempt to lead the stopping in any way, or to consciously indicate that they intend to stop. The trick is to sense when the whole group is ready to stop. If the team is finding it difficult to stop all together, then encourage them to focus their attention on the movement of themselves and their colleagues.

Once the team has been successful at stopping all together at the same time on several occasions then you can attempt the next level. Again, the aim is for the team to stop still all together, but this time, add in a jump.

When everyone is still, the team should attempt to jump (once) all together at the same time. Again, try to avoid obvious cues, but just feel when it is the right time to jump. Once the jump is achieved the team can move off again (together) and mill around once more. The jump only needs to be small, but if any team members don't feel able to jump then replace this with a clap (try to avoid huge arm movements if you are using this version).

82

Of course, this is not magic! As the team members pay full attention to each other and focus on the here and now, their awareness becomes heightened and they pick up on very subtle non-verbal cues from their colleagues.

Exercises for every day

Word at a time stories as a group
Get the team to sit in a circle or any other formation where there is a clear order.

The first person says one word, then the second person says one word and so on. For example, once – upon – a – time – there – was – a – small – chicken. These can be about anything or about a set topic relevant to the team.

Aim for a flow of words, so encourage team members to not think for too long, but to just say what comes into their head.

Always attempt to make sense, i.e. don't be ungrammatical on purpose!

Keep going until the end of the story. Everyone will know when it is – as humans we are well versed in narrative, and have a sense of beginning, middle and end without having to think about it.

This exercise is great practice at not being in charge, relinquishing control of the story to the will of the group as a whole. Some people initially find it very frustrating that they cannot direct the story, or get upset that the story takes a different turn to the one they think it ought to. Urge them to persevere and to enjoy the surprise of not knowing what will come next. This exercise can also be done in pairs, whilst promenading around the room – this is Harry's favourite! If using this version, then swap pairs after each story, so people share the exercise with different colleagues.

One to twenty
The team stands in a close circle looking downwards to the centre. The idea is to count from 1 to 20 in sequence without speaking over each other.

There are no rules about who should speak when or how many times. As a member of the team you should aim to contribute at least one number to the sequence (or you are essentially abandoning any responsibility for the team task). If two people attempt to say the same number, then the team starts again at 1. Harry and Julia regularly do this exercise before performances; it is very settling, requiring focus and connection between all team members. Try not to rush or snatch the words.

Exercises for away days or workshops

You can be more playful and spend more time working on specific areas for your team. Use any of the communication and creativity exercises from previous chapters plus some of the following exercises to create stronger connections between team members and to work on 'group mind'.

Yes, let's!
This is a great warm-up exercise, and it also gets the group into a positive frame of mind and starts the process of working together.

The group members stand anywhere in the space and someone starts by shouting out an action or activity for the group to perform preceded by 'let's', for example, 'Let's stand on one leg!'

The rest of the team shouts 'yes, let's', and performs the action.

As soon as the action is completed, then another team member shouts out another action as it occurs to them, e.g. 'Let's all go and look out the window!'

All other group members respond by shouting out, 'yes, let's' and performing the action suggested.

The exercise doesn't have to be loud, but it must be enthusiastic and positive. Suggestions can build on the previous one or be something new, it doesn't matter. For example, following on from looking out of the window, there could be the suggestion 'Let's name everything we can see out loud', or equally it could be 'Let's all go and touch the door handle'. Initially, some individuals may be reluctant or report that they can't think of anything, so encourage all suggestions.

Some suggestions lend themselves to being carried out for longer than others: if there is a good view out of the window, the team could happily name things they can see for quite a while. Other suggestions are more immediately 'complete', such as standing on one leg.

As the team gets more confident with this exercise, they can escalate the complexity of the suggestions, for example 'Let's all walk around the room doing an impression of Groucho Marx' or 'Let's all pat our heads and rub our stomachs whilst singing the national anthem'.

LISTEN! SAY YES! COMMIT!

The level of silliness of the suggestions will probably vary with the team, how well they already know each other and to some extent the location of the event.

Keep going for as long as you like and/or until everyone is laughing.

Playground game

This exercise is in some ways an advanced version of the previous, and should not be attempted until you are sure that the team is comfortable with each other and with being relatively uninhibited and silly.

The object of this exercise is to create a playground-style game that everyone joins in with. Each time, it is a totally new game that has never been played before. Always remember – the game is created by playing it, not by talking about it. Team members should adopt a child-like mentality and think 'yes and' as much as possible.

The new game starts by someone initiating something: this could be an action, or a vocal command or expression, or both. So, the first person might shout 'brandy butter' and turn around on the spot.

At this point, the other participants have many options as to how they join in: some might join the first person and also shout 'brandy butter' and turn around on the spot. Others might decide to shout 'Brussels sprouts' and turn around in the opposite direction, and others might join them.

So far there may be no obvious 'rules' of the game, but these will emerge as play continues.

For example, someone from the Brussels sprouts participants, noticing that there are more of them than brandy butter participants, shouts 'Christmas cracker' and points accusingly at the other group. The brandy butter participants (picking up on the implication of the gesture) say 'oh no' disappointedly, and all line up against the wall as if they are out of the game.

Of course, almost anything else could have happened instead. And that's the point of this game.

For the first run through, it is a good idea if the facilitator calls a 'time out' as soon as it seems that some rules have emerged, and carries out a short debrief. Ask the participants what they think the rules of the game are, whether it is clear how to win or lose. Certainly on the first go, they may not all agree, but they will realise that they have been able to create at least the semblance of a game. Start again with a brand new game. Although there may have been some 'legs' on the first one, starting a totally new game reinforces the idea that there is an endless supply of new games to be invented – which indeed there is!

Use this exercise carefully. It requires a reasonably high level of comfort within the group. Sometimes the group will get it immediately and create a wonderful game that everyone understands quite quickly. If this happens, play the game again immediately, so everyone can experience the joy of having created something from nothing together. Some days this won't happen! If this exercise isn't resonating with that group on that day, then move on to another exercise. But also, don't give up too soon – if you have committed to doing this exercise, persist for a while.

Point-a-story

This game is great for listening and relinquishing control. It can be played with any number of people, but four to eight works best. If you have more people than that, split the group. Each half can play in turn while the other half acts as the audience.

Arrange the participants into a neat formation so that the 'conductor' can sit in front of them, for example with half the players sitting and half standing behind. The idea is for the group to tell one story by taking turns with the narrative.

The audience suggests a central character. This can be a real person, but if so, it should be someone who is remote from the team such as a famous pop star, or figure from history. (Certainly avoid anyone who is in the room.) Better still just choose a random name, e.g. Fred, so the main character is fictional.

Now, ask the audience 'What is Fred's goal in life?', to which they may say ' to marry Imelda' or 'to climb Mount Everest'. Finally, ask them what's stopping him achieving this goal (or what obstacle he needs to overcome to achieve it).

The conductor points at one of the participants and they start the story. After a few sentences, the conductor points to another participant who carries on the story from exactly where the previous person left off. Ideally, this should be precise, so if the first person is mid-sentence or even mid-word, the next person picks it up.

For example:

Person 1: Fred was out walking one day when he realised that there was a stone in his pocket. He felt it carefully; it was smooth and fitted into the palm of his... (conductor points to someone else)

Person 2: ...hand in a comforting way. Then he took the stone out of his pocket and looked at it. It was...

Person 3: ...suddenly larger as if it was growing. Fred looked around and quickly threw the rock into a bin....

Things to remember:

- The conductor keeps their arm up and pointing all the time, so it is always clear who is supposed to be speaking.
- It is better if the stories are told in the third person (he, she, they).
- As with word-at-a-time stories, participants should aim to always be grammatical and for sentences to make sense. It doesn't matter if they make a mistake, but encourage them to listen hard, so these are minimised.
- The story should be as seamless as possible between participants – the next participant should not repeat the last word or phrase, but should carry on. The effect should be as if one person were reading from a book.
- It doesn't matter whether the story focuses on Fred's achievement of his goal or not. The purpose of the suggestions is to get the group started.
- It is usually clear when it's the end of the story, but if it is going on for too long without obvious resolution then the conductor can indicate that the participants should round it up by making a circle with their non-pointing hand.

You can also start the story by asking the 'audience' for a suggestion for 'a book that's never been written'.

Freeze-tag
This is an exercise that uses physical positions as the suggestion for scenes, so it is preferable that participants be comfortable having some physical contact with each other.

The participants stand in a circle, then two of them volunteer to stand in the middle. In order to start the game, these two participants flail around a bit creating different physical positions until someone else sees a physical position that they like, and shouts 'freeze'. The participants freeze, and then begin a scene that is inspired by the physical positions they are in.

For example, if one has their arm straight up in the air and the other is standing with their hands on their hips, then the first participant might say: 'I didn't see his face officer, but he was about this tall.'

The second participant then assumes the role they have been given and responds as a police officer: 'That's really very tall sir. I find it hard to believe that the burglar managed to escape through that bathroom window [gestures to the window].'

'Oh, he was tall, officer, but this thin [indicates how thin by putting both hands out in front of himself a few inches apart].'

This scene could carry on further, but whenever they feel like it, one of the watching participants shouts 'freeze'. The two participants in the middle stop talking and physically freeze. The participant who shouted then decides which participant they will replace and taps them on the shoulder. They then take over that participant's physical position as exactly as they can, and begin a whole new scene.

The exercise should be quite pacey, so don't leave any one scene going for too long. Also, challenge participants to shout 'freeze' without necessarily having an idea in mind. It is best if you can step into the physical position and then see what idea this inspires.

Note that the person who has shouted 'freeze' and taken over one of the positions is responsible for initiating the next scene. If two people shout 'freeze' at the same time, then both participants in the centre can be replaced at the same time and either person can initiate.

Bodyguard/enemy or Safety zone
Everyone in the room spreads out. Instruct everyone to choose (in their head) one other person in the room to be their 'bodyguard' and one other person to be their 'enemy'. Don't tell anyone your choices. Now, everyone should move to keep their bodyguard between themselves and their enemy. Watch chaos ensue!

This illustrates how each person in a dynamic system influences everyone else through their actions and choices. It's also quite good fun!

Chairs
Place as many chairs as participants around the room. Everyone except one participant sits on a chair, leaving one empty.

The remaining person is 'the zombie', or 'it', and must get to the empty chair to become part of the team again. They start from the opposite end of the room from the empty chair and can only walk like a zombie, i.e. slowly with knees together.

The task of the team is to prevent the zombie from reaching an empty chair by moving seats; they can all move normally, i.e. quickly, but must not talk. If the zombie sits down on an empty chair, whoever is standing up or last moved becomes 'it', and the game is re-set.

This exercise is great for demonstrating to the team the importance of working together. Generally what happens is that the zombie makes it to the empty chair quite easily the first couple of times as team members either don't have the courage to move, or do so in an uncoordinated way. After a few tries however, people usually work out that they need to pay attention to each other and then they can create an effective strategy for preventing the zombie reaching an empty chair.

Chapter 5: LISTEN! SAY YES! COMMIT! Work on Leadership

Here are some definitions of 'lead':

* To guide by going in front
* To cause others to go with one while moving forward

Here are some definitions of 'leader':

* A person who plans, listens and asks questions, supports, represents and advocates, organises, makes decisions, takes actions and takes control on behalf of a group of other people
* A person followed by others
* A person in authority

And here are some definitions of 'leadership':

* A process of social influence in which one person or a small group of people organises and enlists the aid and support of others in the accomplishment of common goals or tasks
* Behaviour associated with a set of individual traits: intelligence, extraversion, openness to experience, adjustment, conscientiousness, self-efficacy and a drive to succeed or complete tasks

Leadership can be complex and hard. Some people seem naturally and intuitively to become authentic leaders without previous experience, practice or training, but not many. Most people eventually take on some kind of leadership role, even if only as parents, and many people report that leadership becomes more effective with practice but seldom feels easy.

In work, people often move into leading teams after gaining some experience and expertise in doing the team's tasks themselves. For many, they start leading 'from cold', without considering the differences between doing work and directing and supporting other people doing work.

Taking on responsibility for other people takes time and energy. Many new leaders begin by saying something like: 'You'll see me every day. I'll be in your face all the time. You'll be sick of the sight of me.' They make a commitment to stay in the 'open mode'. But whatever their hopes or plans at first, after a month or two many find themselves in the 'closed mode', entrenched in their offices, arriving first in the morning and leaving last in the evening, just trying to get through all their inbox and email. If they are seen about at all, they stop making eye contact and move on before their people can have a proper conversation with them, even about vitally important work matters.

Leaders fail when then stop listening, when they reject, undermine, blame or bully their people (examples of passive-aggressive behaviour), when they fail to recognise, accept or work with the situation they are in, or the relationship they have with their teams. They get stuck in their own concerns, stop listening or trying to listen, reject the insights and the ideas of their people and subtly disconnect from the reality of their organisation. This, in improv language, is blocking and denial, and is the exact opposite of the kind of authenticity

94

that leaders need to aim for. We'll talk more about this later on.

There are more specific leadership challenges in the 21st-century workplace:

- Dealing with large amounts of information and the short time-scales. Technology is enabling far more information to be shared and, since the 'lag time' between sending and receiving information has diminished to almost nothing, there is an underlying assumption that decisions can be made and actions taken much faster than in the past.
- Leading diverse groups and teams. People travel widely now and organisations recruit just as widely. Employees are no longer drawn from small homogeneous communities.
- Leading virtual teams. Leaders and team members may seldom or never meet in person, but instead interact only through technology.
- Leading in complex, ambiguous matrix environments. Organisations have moved away from hierarchical structures where leadership is aligned with line management. Now leaders frequently direct and support people they do not manage, and people work in a number of different teams for a number of different leaders simultaneously.
- Leading during organisational change. Change is a constant in most organisations. Changes can range from large and highly impactful through to small and negligible, and from rigorously and thoroughly planned through to completely unplanned. Peoples' reactions to change in work can vary from acceptance, engagement and advocacy, through lack of interest and complacency, to opposition, moaning and even outright sabotage.

- Leading in different working or organisational cultures. Organisations seem to be recruiting their leaders more widely than always 'promoting from within'. This means that leaders can find themselves working in environments where the assumptions and 'default' behaviours are not what they are used to or expect.

- Leading in other countries and (national) cultures. Large numbers of people travel to other countries to work as expatriates and guest workers. Many do so to earn more money and to gain more experience and responsibility than they would in their home country, and they often bring with them the assumptions about leadership that they gained there.

- Leading large groups and whole organisations. The kind of leadership that most people experience in families and small groups does not really equip them for leading large groups and whole organisations. Such a large quantitative difference in group size amounts to a qualitative difference in the leadership role.

...and of course there are different challenges in leading in different business sectors: commercial organisations vs. the public sector vs. government vs. charities, the voluntary sector and non-governmental organisations (NGOs).

All of the challenges listed above can be approached or tackled better when leaders behave in an authentic manner. We talk more about authenticity below, but for now, just treat it as thinking, acting and speaking in the moment. This is hard if we work to an internal script and self-censor all the time.

How can improv help?

It's worth briefly reviewing published research into the efficacy of practicing improvisational skills.

We have already shown that training in improvising techniques has demonstrated impacts, contributing to improved team performance and subsequent innovation (Vera and Crossan, see Chapter 3) as well as improving the team climate for work group innovation (Kirsten, see Chapter 4). Dow et al. (2007) demonstrated that delivering theatre-skills workshops to trainee doctors resulted in a significant improvement in their clinical empathy skills and more recently, Tabaee (2013) studied the impact of improvisation training on leadership skills and has developed a model of improvisational leadership (see the boxed section in this chapter). Her thesis outlines the importance of being able to improvise in today's fast-moving and uncertain business environment and to feel confident making decisions 'in the moment'.

Most of the leading business schools in the US now teach improvisation skills as a core module on their MBAs (see CNN link) and any number of TED talks are available on the subject (see ted.com).

The skills that are developed through practising improvisation have been likened to mindfulness as effective improvisation depends on 'being attentive and alert to what is happening in the now' (Vera and Crossan, 2005). Mindfulness has received much attention recently and has been linked to improved psychological wellbeing, increased adaptability and awareness of emotion (Giluk, 2009). There is also a strong link with the concept of 'flow' (Csikszentmihalyi, 1990), as the merging of action and

LISTEN! SAY YES! COMMIT!

awareness during improvisation is conducive to entering a flow state.

Authentic leadership

Harry and Julia are interested in how improvisation can impact on people's potential for 'authentic leadership'. Here's what we mean by authenticity in this setting:

'Leader behaviour that draws upon and promotes positive psychological capacities, and a positive ethical climate that nourishes self-awareness, an internalised moral perspective, balanced processing of information and relational transparency' (Walumbwa et al., 2008).

'Authenticity is knowing, and acting on, what is true and real inside yourself, your team and your organization AND knowing and acting on what is true and real in the world' (Terry, 1993).

'A process whereby leaders become self-aware of their values, beliefs, identity, motives and goals' (Gardner et al., 2005)

'Being yourself – more – with skill' (Goffee and Jones, 2006)

Goffee and Jones (2006) have an elegant theory of how authenticity can interact with interpersonal skills. They argue that in order to be effective leaders, people need to both be authentic and use high-level interpersonal skills. Without the interpersonal skills, authentic people become 'maverick' leaders, often effective but so at odds with social norms that they can alienate as many people as they win over. But without authenticity, people who are merely socially skilled can appear insincere, not genuine, lacking in integrity. Meanwhile, those with neither authenticity nor social skills can be hopelessly unaware and clumsy around others, i.e. not leaders at all.

These effective leaders and mavericks look a lot like some of the charismatic, dynamic and visionary leaders we mentioned above. And they can be great when organisations are going through transformational (large-scale, planned) change. But an awful lot of leadership involves initiating and controlling small-scale and even unplanned processes and change, everyday stuff. How do leaders balance the transformational leadership thing when there's so much transactional managerial stuff to contend with?

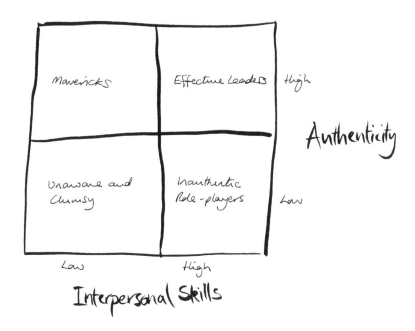

Hersey and Blanchard's Situational Leadership model

Harry and Julia like Hersey and Blanchard's Situational Leadership model (2001). It's another two-factor/four-box model with the underlying ideas that different team members have different needs, that people and relationships can change over time and that good leaders change their behaviour accordingly. It's a model that describes both leaders and team members.

The model suggests that team members can be usefully assessed along two scales: their competence at any particular task, and their commitment in undertaking that task. Leaders can base their own behaviour on this assessment of their team members; the more competent a team member, the less the leader needs to be directive in their style. Similarly, the more committed the team member, the less supportive the leader needs to be.

So team members start as incompetent but committed, and leaders respond by being highly directive but less supportive. Then, as team members' competence increases (and they start to realise their mistakes and so lose commitment), leaders react by becoming coaches: still directive but more supportive. Team members continue to get better at their tasks, so leaders slacken their direction off still further but increase their support. Until finally, team members are fully competent and committed once more, and leaders can delegate and step back to put their energies and attention elsewhere.

This model is great. It demonstrates that leaders do not have to, indeed should not, treat everyone the same in order to be fair. Instead we need to monitor the people, tasks, situations and relationships around us and respond accordingly, dialling up or down our direction and our support of other people as necessary.

So, how do we learn to monitor others in terms of their competence and commitment? How do we widen our portfolio of behaviours in the face of changing situations?

And how do we do this while being effective, authentic and action-centred leaders?

WE IMPROVISE! As we've said, Harry and Julia see leadership as a combination of communication (LISTEN!), creativity (SAY YES!) and teamworking (COMMIT!), so all the previous chapters' advice on why improv helps could be repeated here. Instead we'll just summarise:

Practising improv gives leaders a chance to 'go in front' of others without much risk of failure. They get the chance to communicate, direct (endow) and support others, make decisions and take actions in public and under scrutiny, but in a safe(ish) and supportive environment.

They practise staying in the open mode, initiating, controlling and evaluating actions, while dealing with large amounts of new and changing information in real time and in an ambiguous and mildly threatening context.

They practise working with and understanding a diverse selection of people who are not like them and can directly learn that working with such people increases flexibility and creativity. They can build teams with a sense of 'group mind' who like, trust and respect each other.

They practise 'being themselves', being authentic in front of others, not consciously planning or rehearsing scripts but trying things out and observing their own choices and behaviour. (And reflecting on them, but not too much!) They learn that you don't HAVE to be charismatic, dynamic or visionary to make a difference.

They practise widening their portfolio of behaviours, extending the range of decisions and actions they can make without becoming inauthentic or 'stressy'.

LISTEN! SAY YES! COMMIT!

Exercises leaders can run with their teams

You can introduce these exercises to your regular team meetings, or try them out with a group of willing colleagues during Away Days.

Role-play

Pretty much everyone who has ever attended a training course has participated in or watched some role-play. Many people dislike the thought of it and the experience can be worse, boring or excruciating. But practising behaviour away from the workplace is often the only preparation for doing it for real. It's necessary and better than the alternative (doing it with no preparation or practice at all). Hopefully, starting role-play with three-line conversations and other unthreatening and enjoyable (but powerful) improv exercises will help leaders and their teams learn from them without too much angst.

The point here is for the leaders to practise leading their teams through examples of appropriate and inappropriate behaviour, and using these role-plays as triggers for discussions and decision making about behaviour in work.

Machines and modelling processes with people

Organisational processes and procedures can be pretty dry. How do leaders and their teams get to understand and simplify the flow of information between them, or gain new insight into how a machine or an operation actually works? Make the team into the machine.

As already described in the Creativity chapter, each team member plays a particular component, while the leader (the input or raw material that will be changed by the operation) moves between them. Talk through the process with each component. Once everybody understands what they do, ask how to make the process faster, simpler, better. Try out the suggested improvements. Discuss them. Use the insight gained to improve the actual processes.

Facilitate or run an improv session
Running improv workshops is easier than leading teams and the consequences of failure are less serious. But it still requires plenty of attention, intelligence, deep thinking, communication skills and commitment: great practice for the real world.

Workshop exercises on leadership
There's so much improv that can help leaders. We'll look at a few conversation- and character-based exercises first, and then at a grab-bag of others.

Three-line conversations
These are the raw materials of all improvisational comedy. And as they are no more than short conversations, they can be seen as the raw materials of relationships too.

Two people have a short conversation. Person A says something to person B. Person B responds to person A. Person A responds to person B's response. That's it. So far so simple.

There are plenty of rules of thumb to make the conversations more interesting, more authentic, more funny. Remind participants to start with a blank mind and nothing pre-planned. Understand that whatever is said becomes true the moment it is said. Tell them to listen to their partner, say yes, and commit to the reality they create with what they say. (So, if one person says 'Welcome aboard, Admiral Juan Marcos. Your cabin is ready. We will submerge in 15 minutes', the other person is Spanish (or Latino), an admiral, and is on a submarine.)

Remind them to ease the load on their partners by making statements rather than asking questions, or only to ask questions if they add new information to the conversation. Stop and restart the conversations if participants encounter problems or confusion ('Oh is that what I am?'), or deny or block the reality that is being created. ('This isn't a submarine, it's a brothel, and I've brought the sandwiches.')

Suggest that participants assume that they already know everything about their partner and the situation they are in. ('Thank you Miguel. You look a little hot. I take it that the carbon dioxide scrubbers have not yet been fully repaired.')

Clearly, this is only a heuristic, a rule of thumb, not an algorithm, an absolute law. It doesn't work all the time: we can all think of situations where 'pretending we understand when we don't and going with the flow' can be disastrous. For example, hearing and accepting a three-letter acronym without clarifying what it means, on the basis that you will be able to work it out later, can be dangerous; especially when you can go on to use it incorrectly, or in the wrong situation.

Thing is, many organisations complain of 'analysis paralysis', a culture mired in meetings and emails full of questions and explanations. Top teams and their managers don't want to act until their backs are covered. Practising saying yes in a safe and consequence-free improv setting, accepting people and situations immediately on face value, can show us that this can be useful sometimes in the real world too. That 'sometimes' is vital: as well as practising saying yes, we need to practise spotting the times and places where it's appropriate to do so, when lives and money and reputations are not at risk.

Back to three-line conversations...

Make sure that participants concentrate on listening to and supporting their partners rather than being funny or clever themselves.

Tell them to try not to be a 'talking head' at a safe one-metre distance from their partner. Encourage them to do something unlike their typical behaviour, to mix things up a bit:

- 'Stack' your body differently as you enter.
- Take your hands out of your pockets.
- Make a non-verbal 'human' noise before speaking.
- Grab an imaginary object as you begin the conversation (and find out what it is, then use it, or don't use it, during the conversation).
- Touch your scene partner as you speak.
- React with extreme emotion to what your scene partner says.
- Try reacting without intelligible words, or using gibberish.
- Undertake an activity during the scene, without talking about it at all.

If participants have the mental bandwidth, they can try to enrich the conversation with additional subtle information. They can have a secret want that they don't mention or indicate but which influences their actions (I just want to be hugged. I want to find out how much they earn...). They can be a 'stock character' in a movie, TV or book genre (moll, grass, robot, patsy, principal boy etc.). Or an archetype (warrior, lover, magician etc.). They can impersonate someone they love or hate, someone known to them, a celebrity or a fictional character.

Keep moving the participants around, so that each conversation starts afresh between new people.

Three-line conversations can be immensely rich and as they are quick, you can do a lot of them in a relatively short time. It's possible to treat them like Amateur Dramatics and go for surface laughs. But for leadership development purposes, they are more useful when you go for depth. Try to dig out aspects of the participants that people don't often see and which are less familiar: have fun but step carefully!

Often, when people start doing improv they feel that everything they do is mad, perverse or (worse) mundane and boring. Embrace this and keep going to discover what else people come up with. Doing extended sessions of three-line conversations can feel a little like the 'Hell Week' that Special Forces soldiers go through: breaking participants down in order to explore what's at the core, and then working out again from that.

Longer two- and three-person conversations

Once people start stringing three-line conversations together, they start having role-plays, and these can be as rich and as deep as you and your participants want. All the above rules of thumb apply, and if the role-play is happening in front of other participants, make sure you cut pretty quickly: don't leave people to squirm in an embarrassing situation. Cut on the first big laugh (or life lesson!).

In improv performance, players are often advised against creating a 'plot monster'. This is where something so huge is introduced into a scene that everything else has to hinge on its resolution. For example, if an audience sees a character as a man and then after a time jump sees them again as a woman, the audience will expect to find out how the transition happened. Working through this amount of plot is likely to kill off any other improvisations that players may bring in. If it works it can be very satisfying, but, in the hands of inexperienced improvisers, it often doesn't.

However, plot monsters can be useful for organisational improvisation in workshops. How do we turn the company green? How do we cope with a merger or acquisition? How do we drastically improve the bottom-line performance? How do we manage massive transformational change? Improv can provide a safe and consequence-free setting to think the unthinkable, say the unsayable and do almost anything. And in a workshop, where everyone is a participant and there is no separate audience, it doesn't matter if there's no neat and tidy resolution.

More structured exercises

Blank workplace
This is really no more than a succession of three-line conversations, but in a classic comedic 'Set up – Set up – Twist' format. It pretty much always gets a laugh, but can touch on real truths too.

Four people take part, two 'on stage' and one in each 'wing'. The workshop facilitator asks the rest of the group to suggest an emotion. Then the two people on stage have a short conversation where they don't name the emotion but where everything they do is imbued with the emotion. The third person enters the conversation and attempts to ramp up the emotion still more. The fourth person enters and makes an announcement or initiates a new conversation, in which they embody the complete opposite of the emotion seen up to now. Everyone laughs.

For example, a Blank Workplace, given the suggestion of 'Honesty at the Admin Office' could result in:

Jane: I hate this job. I've never said it before Brian, but I do.

Brian: Since you're opening up to me, I must tell you that I used your stapler yesterday and I broke it. Sorry.

Jane: Oh. OK. I accept your apology. And I'm sorry I ate your Stilton out of the Fridge.

Brian: That's OK Jane. You can eat my cheese anytime because… Well, I have to tell you I love you.

Derek: Hello Jane and Brian. I'm not supposed to tell you this but Peterson is about to sack everyone.

Jane: Oh no! Here he comes! Peterson hates us.

Peterson: Hello, my favourite three people in the office. Really good news about the quarterly results…

This exercise helps us to read others, to express emotions clearly, to boil messages down to simple unambiguous elements. And the quality being explored needn't just be an emotion; it could be one of the organisational values (or their opposite), or a characteristic of a particular function or department.

Status games

These are a series of three-line conversations, usually between two people. The workshop facilitator can get suggestions for job titles or relationships between the participants, and in addition suggests (openly or secretly) the relative status of the participants, i.e. higher or lower.

We recognise a number of simple behaviours as higher status: holding yourself erect; holding your head still; speaking with a deeper and more sonorous voice; speaking less; making prolonged eye contact; making slow controlled movements. Lower status often looks like: cramped, pinched or closed postures; fast and uncontrolled movements especially of the eyes, head and hands; high or otherwise strained voices; lots of words and sub-vocalisations.

Johnstone (1981) wrote what is probably the definitive work on status for actors: he argues that, in order to function as social animals, humans continually attempt to monitor and manage their standing in the 'pecking order'. In traditional hierarchical businesses this was probably pretty straightforward, but in today's cross-functional, virtual, matrix organisations it can be a full-time job and a source of stress.

Acting out and observing simple 'Master Servant' scenarios can help people see where their behaviour is still driven by the traditional hierarchies. Practising playing unfamiliar high or low status roles, can widen participants' behavioural vocabularies. More fun can be had when participants compete to go for higher or lower status. Or when they are briefed to change status over the duration of the scene.

Leaders usually need to be able to assume a higher status. But acting higher status does not always come naturally. And senior people need to be able to drop their status in order to apologise and be contrite. Practice can help, especially as participants start to relax and play more with status. Is it better to make some requests as low-status rather than high-status people? How do you deal with the person who won't move off their low-status or high-status position?

As Johnstone argued, exploring status is a powerful means to make good actors even better. As such, Harry and Julia have found it rather 'too rich' for one-off workplace learning events. But an exploration of status can be useful when working with highly able individuals or teams as part of an extended development programme.

The following exercises are less based on conversation or character.

Museum curator
Participants wander round the training room. Each in term takes the role of museum curator, introducing the group to the hidden wonders and little-known history of the everyday objects found in the room.

This is no more than simple practice at making stuff up and bullshitting. Stringing sentences together on the fly and making some kind of sense talking in public is a real skill that all leaders need to practise. Harry and Julia don't recommend that you do too much reflection or analysis of your performance in this exercise when you finish. Just let people pitch into it with an intention to keep the talk going, and observe themselves while they do it. If big conclusions jump out, then by all means follow them, but don't be worried if this just feels OK.

Press conference

Similar to Museum Curator but with much more inbuilt threat and tension.

One participant is the press representative launching some new product, service or idea to the other participants who are all playing journalists.

The PR person needs to stay on message, stay civil and answer the questions of the journalists. The journalists' brief is to get the wrong end of the stick and repeatedly question the PR person on some trivial, inconsequential and ideally wrong-headed aspect of the PR person's presentation. If all the journalists hound the PR person on a single issue it's even funnier. So:

PR: Thank you everybody. I'll be focusing today on the introduction of new organic pigments to Colour Me Happy Ltd's top selling brands of paint. The red...

1st Journo: Mike Spreader, Farming Today. So are all the pigs branded?

PR: Thanks Mike. No: there are no pigs. As I was saying, the red...

2nd Journo: Arabella Field, Agriculture News. So I take it that you've moved the entirety of your pig farming operation overseas? What about the loss of revenue to UK farmers?

PR: Hi Arabella. Let's get back on track shall we. These organic colours... etc.

This is a fun version of a real leadership challenge: presenting an idea to a group and dealing with the misunderstandings and questions that naturally result. Practice for situations that can often go wrong in real life.

Story line

An interesting one this, all about understanding and constructing narrative. Leaders need to be able to tell their story along with those of their teams and organisations. They also need to be able to understand and interpret the stories told by others.

A group of five to eight participants take part. Any others in the session become the audience.

The first participant takes a 'stage right' position facing the others and is given the first line of a story (suggested by the audience) which they repeat. They need to remember it so they can repeat it often.

Another participant takes a 'stage left' position and is given and repeats the last line of the story. The last line need not have any particular connection to the first (for now) but it also needs to be remembered so that it can be repeated.

The first and last lines can have as much significance to the group and the organisation as you want. ('Once upon a time Acme Ltd wanted to merge with its largest competitor'... 'And so the united organisation exceeded its productivity and profitability targets for many years.')

One after another, the other participants join in and fill in the gaps (verbally) between the first and last lines, while simultaneously taking the appropriate position between their fellows. Their job is to fill out the story, introducing the major plot points. Each time a new person joins the story line, all the lines are repeated in order.

This is a very satisfying and often very funny way to explore narrative and storytelling. It can relate to Kenn Adams' Story Spine idea (1991) too, that says that all stories follow a similar model:

Once upon a time there was <a protagonist>...
And every day...
Until one special day...
So because of that...
And because of that...
And because of that...
Until, finally...
And ever since then...

Joseph Campbell's (1949) book is the definitive work on the power and sense of narrative; it is still in use today.

More recently Rhodes and Brown (2005) have published a useful summary of recent theory and research into narrative in organisations, if you want to know more.

Colour advance
This is another storytelling exercise, great for creating, examining or fixing the organisational narrative or its values, vision, mission and overall strategic objectives.

People work in pairs, managed by a workshop facilitator, in front of other session participants. They tell a story together, where one person speaks at a time and can have either a few words or many sentences to say before the other person takes over.

Each of them has a very specific role. One has the responsibility for advancing the story by focusing on plot and action and can (indeed, should) gloss over detail as

113

much as possible. The other colours in the details through exhaustive description and may not progress the plot at all.

The workshop facilitator indicates who speaks when by commanding 'COLOUR!' or 'ADVANCE!' Sometimes the workshop facilitator gets the pair to swap roles.

This is useful as a way to demonstrate and practise the kind of 'helicopter vision' needed in leadership. People with a tendency to micro-manage have the opportunity to learn to advance, leaving the details to others. People who more naturally focus on theory can learn to look closer, reflect and describe. Participants learn their own preference and practise switching roles. And the content of the stories can be as serious and non-trivial as you like.

Super managers
This is a silly game, familiar from *Whose Line is it Anyway?* on TV, which is useful as an energy booster and warm-up during leadership events.

The workshop facilitator invites the participants to suggest a work or even world problem, and a (completely unrelated) super power, as silly and inconsequential, as they like. The first person up has the super power and acts it out while talking about solving the problem.

They invite the second participant up while endowing them with a new, unconnected and equally random super power. The second participant joins the first, has a three-line conversation about the problem, then invites the third, on the same terms. And so on for up to eight participants.

Then, in reverse order, the super managers find reasons to leave, until eventually the first participant is left, with the problem solved or unsolved, whatever.

Leadership exercises you can do by yourself

Elevator pitch, or Cocktail party chat

This has already been described in Chapter 2, but here you are exhorted to do it by yourself! Say:

- What are you working on at the moment?
- What's your department/function/team/organisation for?

The point of this practice is NOT to develop a script or plan. Rather, it's about listening to your own approach and reflecting on how to concentrate on the most important elements of your stories.

Remember:

- No planning in advance
- Listen to yourself non-judgementally
- Repeat, but don't look for incremental or organic improvement – that would mean you were developing a script. Try to keep it different every time.

Feature: Improvisational Leadership

Farnaz Tabaee's doctorate (2013) examined the effects of improvisation techniques in leadership development. The author suggested that adaptive decision-making techniques are increasingly required in today's complex and ambiguous business world, and that managers and leaders are more frequently required to improvise solutions, but without any training in how to adopt an improvisational mindset effectively. Her research involved the delivery of workshops to groups of leaders and managers to introduce them to the principles of improvisation, and to give them experience of applying these principles through improv exercises. Her results suggest that participants acquired more effective listening skills, but more importantly that the experience of improvising resulted in an increase in their willingness to take 'competent risks', to celebrate failure and use mistakes to learn when back at work. In addition, participants indicated reduced stress and enhanced mindfulness as a result of attending the workshop.

The Holistic Improvisational Leadership Model was developed from her work and is shown below. It is proposed that the organisational conditions on the left-hand side, which have been shown to be moderating factors in the effectiveness of improvisational approaches (see Vera and Crossan's research in Chapter 4), provide support for the development of the improvisational competencies in the circle, which, in turn, lead to positive organisational outcomes.

Work on Leadership

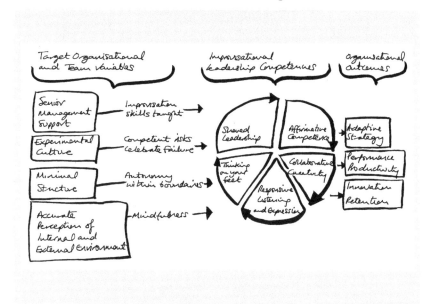

LISTEN! SAY YES! COMMIT!

Here's a bunch of stuff..

…we could have mentioned, but didn't:

- Laughter therapy, laughter yoga et al.
- Maslow and Herzberg's theories
- Forum and Playback theatre
- Contact improvisation or five-rhythms dance
- Relationship of improv to coaching, mentoring and counselling
- Personality theory, especially Extraversion-Introversion
- RAND and the Prisoner's Dilemma
- Johari Window
- Emotional intelligence
- Resilience and mental toughness
- 10,000 hour rule – as described by Malcolm Gladwell

If you are interested in any of these, Google them!

LISTEN! SAY YES! COMMIT!

About the authors

Harry Puckering

I competed in (and won!) public speaking competitions while I was at school, and then acted my way through university, but after that didn't do anything on stage, apart from the odd works party, until about 1999.

In that year I changed my career (from publisher to trainer) and joined the amateur fund-raising pantomime for my daughters' schools. While my kids grew up, my development at work (designing and delivering all manner of personal, management and team development events and programmes), and in pantomime, paralleled each other. Over the next seven years I co-wrote five panto scripts, played three dames, two baddies, a henchman (well, henchrat actually) and the principal girl's best friend.

When the panto ended in 2005, I co-wrote a couple of amateur fund-raising cabaret shows and started attending acting classes at Brighton's New Venture Theatre. A friend in the class, stand-up comedian Adam Smith, recommended a Brighton improv drop-in class run by John Cremer. John's company, the Maydays, soon took over the class and I met most of the city's active improvisers.

Since then I've attended more improv learning and performance events, met Julia and through her joined the Hee-Ha's, another Brighton troupe specializing in short-form shows, who've performed in a number of Brighton Festival Fringes and have regular shows at two Brighton venues:

Otherplace at Bar Broadway and the Dukebox Theatre. I also occasionally run the very same improv drop-in started by John Cremer.

While all that was going on I also played bass in a variety of bands, getting to the point where I am now in the rhythm section of a superb Greek combo, the George Kypreos Band, where although I seldom improvise, I continually support the improvisations of the band's leader, George Kypreos.

Improv started as fun, as relief and respite from being a responsible dad, being planful and professional at work, learning tunes, practising my instrument and learning lines in plays. But I quickly came to see that improv was helping me communicate (and step forward confidently with no plan or script in mind!), be more comfortably flexible, spontaneous and creative, be a more considerate and responsive team member and, I hope, a better and more authentic leader of groups and projects.

For me, improv has become like meditation, enabling me to feel less fearful and more centred in many parts of my life. I hope to pass that on to others in this book and in my work.

Julia E. Knight

I didn't do any acting at school or university, but I did perform as a musician in orchestras, wind bands, choirs and took the occasional solo – I was principal oboist in the Lincolnshire County Youth Orchestra for two years! And I took music exams – lots of them. None of which taught me to improvise, in fact, precisely the opposite. The job of the classical musician is to play what is written on the page. Interpret it, sure, but make stuff up? That is the job of jazz musicians!

I could have gone to music college, but someone helpful told me that one shouldn't pursue one's hobby as a career, because it then becomes work, ergo boring and tedious. So I went to study psychology at what is now Northumbria University, and then a few years later I studied for a Masters degree in Occupational Psychology at the University of Sheffield. After working for a small consultancy and then for The Post Office, I was a Chartered Psychologist and set out into the world of self-employment, as what a colleague calls a 'jobbing psychologist'.

In this freelance land, there is quite a lot of training delivery (and design) on offer. So by the time I moved to Brighton in 2007 I had chalked up many hundreds of hours in front of groups of managers urging them to learn about, among other things, communication skills, presenting, interviewing, managing performance, being assertive and how to administer a psychometric test. The reason for mentioning the training delivery specifically is because I had come to realise that the times I enjoyed most were when I was 'put on the spot' and required to improvise. Perhaps a box of materials didn't show up, or someone in the group posed an unusual question.

So, somehow or other I ended up at a comedy improvisation show in Brighton, and thought 'that looks like the best fun!'. After attending a 10-week beginner's course with The Maydays I realised that I had discovered a passion, and luckily for me so did several of the other people on that course and The Hee-Ha's were formed. Since then there have been five Fringe Festivals, 20 or so different troupe members (coming and going throughout) and more than 50 gigs in pubs, theatres and at people's houses. I now also act as teaching cover for the Maydays when they have other commitments.

LISTEN! SAY YES! COMMIT!

Like Harry, I quickly noticed the relevance of improv to my work. Initially, in the obvious way – improved communication, confidence and mental agility. Later, once I was rehearsing with the Hee-Ha's on a regular basis, I realised the power of improv techniques to create strong team bonds. As a trained scientist, my first instinct is to seek out the evidence, so I started searching for relevant literature in the applied psychology and management journals. Some of it is referred to in this book, but not too much. This isn't supposed to be an evidence evaluation, it's supposed to be a practical book. And that's what I really enjoy – providing practical support for people to help them grow their ability to interact more comfortably and flexibly in the workplace.

Bibliography

Books and Dissertations

Argyris, C. (1985) *Strategy, Change and Defensive Routines.* Boston MA: Pitman Publishing.

Argyris, C. (1999) *On Organizational Learning.* 2nd Ed. Malden MA: Blackwell.

Avolio, B. J. & Luthans, F. (2006) *The high impact leader: Moments matter for accelerating authentic leadership development.* New York: McGraw-Hall.

Campbell, J. (1949) The Hero with a Thousand Faces. New York: Pantheon (Bollingen Series 17).

Campbell, J., Cousineau, P. (ed) (1990) The Hero's Journey: Joseph Campbell on His Life and Work. New York: Harper and Row.

Cooper, C. L. and Argyris, C. (eds) (1998) *The Concise Blackwell Encyclopedia of Management.* Malden, MA: Blackwell Business.

Cremer, J. (2009) *Improv: Enjoy Life and Success with the Power of Yes.* Oxford: Sunmakers.

Csikszentmihalyi, M. (1990) *Flow: The psychology of optimal experience*. New York: Harper & Row.

Flaxman, P. E., Bond, F. W. & Livheim, F. (2013) *The Mindful and Effective Employee: An Acceptance & Commitment Therapy Training Manual for Improving Well-Being and Performance*. Oakland, CA: New Harbinger.

Goffee, R. and Jones, G. (2006) *Why Should Anyone be Led by You?: What it takes to be an Authentic Leader*. Boston, MA: Harvard Business School.

Halpern, C., Close, D. & Johnson, K. (1994) *Truth in Comedy: The manual of improvisation*. Colorado Springs, CO: Meriwether.

Hersey, P., Blanchard, K. H. & Johnson, D. F. (2001) *Management of Organizational Behaviour*. (8th Ed). Upper Saddle River, NJ: Prentice-Hall.

Hough, K. (2011) *The Improvisation Edge: Secrets to Building Trust and Radical Collaboration at Work*. San Francisco, CA: Berrett-Koehler.

Johnstone, K. (1981) *Impro: Improvisation and the Theatre*. London: Eyre Methuen.

Kirsten, B. (2008) *The influence of a team development intervention (improvisational theatre) on climate for work group innovation*. Thesis (MComm (Industrial Psychology)): Stellenbosch University.

Koppett, K. (2001) *Training to Imagine: Practical Improvisational Theatre Techniques to Enhance Creativity, Teamwork, Leadership and Learning*. Sterling, VA: Stylus.

Napier, M. (2004) *Improvise: Scene from the Inside Out*. Chicago: Heinemann.

Poynton, R. (2008) *Everything's an Offer*. Portland, OR: On Your Feet.

Salinsky, T. and Frances-White, D. (2008) *The Improv Handbook: the ultimate guide to improvising in comedy, theatre and beyond*. London: Continuum International Publishing Group.

Schein, E. H. (1985) *Organizational Culture and Leadership*. San Francisco, CA: Jossey-Bass.

Seham, A. (2001) *Whose Improv is it Anyway?* Jackson, MS: University Press of Mississippi.

Tabaee, F. (2013) *Effects of improvisation techniques in leadership development*. PhD dissertation: Pepperdine University. http://gradworks.umi.com/35/62/3562861.html

Terry, R. W. (1993) *Authentic Leadership: Courage in Action*. New York: Jossey-Bass.

West, M. A. & Markiewicz, L. (2004) *Building Team-based Working*. Malden MA: BPS Blackwell.

Wiseman, R. (2009) *59 Seconds: Think a little, change a lot*. London: Macmillan.

Journals and Articles

Corsun D. L. et al. (2006) Overcoming managers' perceptual shortcuts through improvisational theater games. *Journal of Management Development*. 25(4): 298–315.

Dow, A. W. et al. (2007) Using Theater to Teach Clinical Empathy: A Pilot Study. *Journal of General Internal Medicine.* 22(8): 1114–1118.

Gardner, W. L., Avolio, B. J., Luthans, F., May, D. R., & Walumbwa, F. O. (2005). Can you see the real me? A self-based model of authentic leader and follower development. *The Leadership Quarterly.* 16(3): 343–372.

Giluk, T. L. (2009) Mindfulness, Big Five personality, and affect: A meta-analysis. *Personality and Individual Differences.* 47(8): 805–811.

Hayes, S. C. et al. (2006) Acceptance and Commitment Therapy: Model, processes and outcomes. *Behaviour Research and Therapy.* 44(1): 1–25.

Lewis, C. & Lovatt, P. J. (2013) Breaking away from set patterns of thinking: Improvisation and divergent thinking. *Thinking Skills and Creativity.* 9: 46–58.

Limb, C. J. & Braun, A. R. (2008) Neural Substrates of Spontaneous Musical Performance: An fMRI Study of Jazz Improvisation. *PLoS ONE.* 3(2): e1679.

Mirvis, P. (1998) Variations on a Theme—Practice Improvisation. *Organization Science.* 9(5): 586–592.

Moorman, C. and Miner, A. S. (1998) Organizational Improvisation and Organizational Memory. *Academy of Management Review.* 23(4): 698-723

Kamoche, K., Cunha, M. P. e. and Cunha, J. V. d. (2003) Towards a Theory of Organizational Improvisation: Looking Beyond the Jazz Metaphor. *Journal of Management Studies.* 40(8): 2023–2051.

Rhodes, C. and Brown, A. D. (2005) Narrative, organizations and research. *International Journal of Management Reviews.* 7(3): 167–188.

Schyns, B. & Day, D. (2010) Critique and review of leader-member exchange theory. *European Journal of Work and Organizational Psychology.* 19(1): 1–29.

Tannenbaum, R. and Schmidt, W. H. (1973) How To Choose a Leadership Pattern. *Harvard Business Review.* 51(3): 162–180.

Vera, D. and Crossan, M. (2004) Theatrical Improvisation: Lessons for Organizations. *Organization Studies.* 25(5): 727–749.

Vera, D. and Crossan, M. (2005) Improvisation and Innovative Performance in Teams. *Organization Science.* 16(3): 203–224.

Walumbwa, F., Avolio, B., Gardner, W., Wernsing, T. and Peterson, S. (2008) Authentic Leadership: Development and Validation of a Theory-Based Measure. *Journal of Management.* 34(1): 89–126.

Weick, K. E. (1998) Improvisation as a Mindset for Organizational Analysis. *Organization Science.* 9(5): 543–555.

Wiener, D. J. (1999) Using Theater Improvisation to Assess Interpersonal Functioning. *International Journal of Action Methods.* 52(2): 51–69.

Weblinks – e-books – press

CNN Article – Why using improvisation to teach business skills is no joke.
http://edition.cnn.com/2010/BUSINESS/02/18/improvisation.business.skills/index.html

FT Article – Have you heard the one about… (registration required to view)

http://www.ft.com/cms/s/0/3f8f3838-e677-11de-98b1-00144feab49a.html?nclick_check=1

Guardian Article and VT of Fiona Shaw having MRI
http://www.guardian.co.uk/science/2009/nov/24/fiona-shaw-neuroscience

Improv in Business e-book
http://bizimprovlab.files.wordpress.com/2010/12/using-improv-in-business-final-edition-1-02.pdf

Ken Adams Story Spine: see
http://www.aerogrammestudio.com/2013/06/05/back-to-the-story-spine/

Crunchy Frog – Improv in the UK
http://www.thecrunchyfrogcollective.com/

#0073 - 120918 - C0 - 210/148/7 - PB - DID2302503